Cambridge English Readers

Level 5

Series editor: Philip Prowse

Windows of the Mind

Frank Brennan

CAMBRIDGE
UNIVERSITY PRESS

CAMBRIDGE
UNIVERSITY PRESS

University Printing House, Cambridge CB2 8BS, United Kingdom

Cambridge University Press is part of the University of Cambridge.

It furthers the University's mission by disseminating knowledge in the pursuit of education, learning and research at the highest international levels of excellence.

www.cambridge.org
Information on this title: www.cambridge.org/9780521750141

First published 2001
Reprinted 2016

Printed in the United Kingdom by Hobbs the Printers Ltd

A catalogue record for this publication is available from the British Library

ISBN 978-0-521-75014-1 Paperback

Contents

A Fine Wine

'Extraordinary! Quite, quite extraordinary!'

Daniel Appleby did not often use such words to describe the wines he tasted. The other man in the room was waiting to see if he liked this one or not. His future depended on what Daniel Appleby said – if he liked the wine it would be bought by one of the biggest supermarkets around. It would be sold everywhere. The man who owned the vineyard looked on nervously. His vineyard was small, but it was one of the oldest in the Bordeaux region of France. If he sold his wine, the business that had been in his family for over two hundred years would be saved.

Daniel Appleby held the glass to his nose and smelled the wine again. He lifted the glass up to the light from the window to see its colour better. He was the Chief Wine Taster for Happimart Supermarkets. If he liked a wine, then everybody bought it. If he didn't like a wine, nobody did. His word was like the judgement of God.

'You say you have been making this wine for the last two hundred years?' he asked the other man, Monsieur Colbert, a proud-looking man of over seventy years of age, whose hair was still as black as it had been when he was twenty.

'I am old but I am not *that* old, sir,' Monsieur Colbert said with a little smile. 'But my family has been making this wine since the time of Napoleon Bonaparte. If I may say so, this is the only vineyard in all of France to produce wine in this way. It is my secret.'

Monsieur Colbert was hoping that his little joke might relax things a little.

Daniel Appleby took his profession very seriously. He was the best. He never, ever joked when he tasted wine. He might joke about other wine tasters at other times – in fact, he often did. But he never joked *during* a wine tasting. It was too important. *He* was too important. He held the glass up to the light once more and looked at the deep red colour before finally putting the glass onto the table in front of him. He had made up his mind.

'Monsieur Colbert,' he said, as he placed his thumbs into the pockets of the red jacket he wore, the one that matched his tie so well. 'You are to be congratulated: this is an exceptionally fine wine with a strong bouquet and a rich fruity flavour with suggestions of blackcurrant; a wine to go well with any game or red meat, or to be enjoyed on its own for its excellent and strong personality . . .'

Monsieur Colbert smiled with delight. This was just what he had hoped to hear.

'. . . but,' Daniel Appleby went on as he took out his glasses from the pocket of his expensive jacket and put them on again, 'is this the right kind of wine for the customers of Happimart Supermarkets? They are used to wines that cannot compare with this quality. Their tastes are . . . er . . . less well-developed than those of people such as ourselves. I wonder if they would fully enjoy the finer qualities of this remarkable wine? I wonder if they would be prepared to *pay* more for such quality?'

The old man's smile disappeared. Monsieur Colbert was

proud of his wine but he was not a rich man. He had to sell his wine or go out of business. He was getting old and he owed a lot of money. He needed money if he was to retire with his wife, whose health had never been good since their only son, Jacques, had died two years before. This could be their last chance.

'I promise you, Monsieur Appleby, that my wine is worth every franc; there is no better wine of this type in the region!'

Daniel Appleby smiled and picked up the glass again, holding it up against his fleshy nose and allowing the edge of the glass to brush against his neat sandy moustache. He breathed in deeply through his nose and sighed.

'Ah, you are right, Monsieur Colbert – this is one of the best wines I have ever tasted!' He stopped for a moment to think of the numerous examples of wine that had passed his lips. This was by far the finest, none of the others could compare with it. And it would be great to add this to the Happimart wine list, *his* wine list. But it would have to be on his terms, of course.

'But,' he continued, 'there is little demand for expensive fine wines – not in our type of supermarkets. Oh, there are wealthy men who will always pay for quality, that is true. But are there enough, Monsieur Colbert, are there enough? The customer of today is the ordinary shopper, not the rich man. And there are a great many more ordinary shoppers than there are millionaires; the shoppers are the ones who make our money for us, Monsieur, and we have to please them, you can be sure of that.'

'Just what exactly are you saying, Monsieur Appleby? Are you refusing to buy my wine because it is too good?'

asked Monsieur Colbert, his voice showing more anger than he had intended. Times had been bad and his small vineyard had always depended on the high prices that wines of superior quality fetch. But fewer people were prepared to pay for such luxuries now, and he knew that the Englishman from the supermarket was quite aware of this. He didn't want to lose his business completely. He would have to see what he was offered and hope for the best.

'I am saying, Monsieur,' said Appleby, finally, 'that Happimart Supermarkets always try to offer the best value for their customers. *We* are experts at selling for the best prices on the market and *you* are expert at making quality wine. I say we can combine our abilities and offer our customers the finest wines at prices they can afford.'

Monsieur Colbert was not familiar with Appleby's way of doing business. He liked people to be direct and open when they were dealing with him.

'And what exactly are your terms, Monsieur Appleby?' he asked.

Daniel Appleby played with his glass as he spoke, admiring the rich dark colour of the wine as he held it up to the light from the window. He was used to moments like this, and enjoyed them almost as much as the fine wines he loved.

'My terms are the terms Happimart offers to all the smaller vineyards it does business with. We like to see fine wines made, but we are realistic about today's market. We offer to buy your vineyard from you and take the responsibility from your hands, while employing you to be in charge of wine production . . .'

'But Monsieur . . . ?' Monsieur Colbert did not like the sound of the idea.

'Well, naturally we wouldn't expect you to produce the wine by yourself! Our expert production staff would work under your direction. That way you have the best of everything – you continue to make wine but you have the money from the sale of your vineyard and a contract from Happimart, too. A very fine offer, I think you'll agree. . .'

What Appleby didn't mention was that once the 'production staff' had learned everything about Colbert's ways of producing his wine, Happimart would find some reason to get rid of him.

Old Monsieur Colbert spoke again.

'This vineyard has been in my family for generations, Monsieur; it means a lot to me and the honour of my family name. What price are you offering for a wine which was good enough for the Emperor Napoleon himself?'

Daniel Appleby smiled and he named an amount that took the old man's breath away. It was far, far less than old Colbert had hoped for. But it would be just enough to pay back the money he owed and have a little left over. And he would have a job, at least. He would have to retire later than he had wanted to but he was used to working.

Old Colbert recovered himself and spoke. 'Monsieur, will you allow me a few moments alone to think over your offer?'

'Certainly, Monsieur. Take as long as you need, though I will have to leave soon. It would be a pity to go without having our business brought to . . . er . . . a happy conclusion. I will take a walk around your vineyard for a while.'

Daniel Appleby went outside. It was late afternoon. He could see the rows of vines stretching out in the golden light of the sun. He had hardly gone more than a few metres when he stopped. He knew that if his offer was not accepted the old man would lose everything. He would be no different from all the other small wine producers who had failed to meet the demands of the modern market. No different but for one thing: this wine was the finest he had ever tasted and he *had* to be the one to get it.

He got it. Half an hour later the agreement was signed. As Daniel Appleby drove to the airport he carried with him the signed agreement for Happimart's latest buy.

In a room in a chateau in Bordeaux an old man cried.

*   *   *

Daniel Appleby took a taxi from the airport to his expensive flat in London. He was happy with the way things had gone. It had been just like all the other times. Sometimes the small vineyards produced wines that sold well and sometimes they didn't, but Happimart always made money. If the vineyards didn't make enough money Happimart could always sell them again – there was always some way to make money. If the previous owners were not left with any way of making a living it was not Happimart's problem. That was the way of the world.

Daniel Appleby was looking forward to a new future with the Happimart company. He had been invited to be the presenter in a television show Happimart were paying for. It was a show all about food and drink called *Dinner Party*, and he would be the show's expert on wines. He would be able to do what he had always wanted: to spend all of his time eating and drinking the finest food and wine. He would show off his expert knowledge, thoroughly enjoy himself, *and* he would be paid very well.

Yes, he had everything planned. His future looked bright. Soon he would no longer have to taste all the awful cheap wines Happimart usually sold to its stupid customers. He looked at the lights of the city as the evening sun was setting. The sky was yellow and orange and red. It was beautiful.

Unfortunately, he didn't notice the other car as it lost control and crashed into his taxi.

*   *   *

The doctors all agreed that Daniel Appleby was a lucky man. He had hit his head against the taxi door and had been knocked out. The taxi driver had escaped with cuts and bruises. Even the taxi had not been damaged beyond repair. The only sign of the accident left on Daniel was a small cut just above his nose. It could have been a lot worse.

Daniel had to stay in hospital for a day for observation, just to make sure that he was all right. He did not really mind. The only thing Daniel was not looking forward to was hospital food. The food served by hospitals was plain and very different from the kind of cooking he was used to. He did not mind plain food – a nice lobster cooked in its shell, or perhaps a simple steak served with a basic green salad. Maybe just fresh bread with a good cheese and a glass of cool white wine. He was willing to go without when he had to.

When his first meal arrived he was horrified. It was

burger, chips and peas with a glass of orange juice. It looked awful. It tasted worse. Daniel had to call the nurse.

'Nurse,' he told her. 'This burger tastes like salty cardboard, the chips are like soap, the peas are tasteless and hard and the orange juice is like old vinegar! Don't you have any *fresh* food here? Are you trying to play some kind of joke on me or what?'

The nurse took away the food and he was brought a salad instead. Once again, Daniel Appleby complained that his food had no proper taste. The nurse had the food checked by the manager of the kitchen. The manager said it all tasted fine.

'That manager's tongue must be made out of rubber,' Daniel replied in disgust.

The doctor was called and tests were made immediately on Daniel to see if anything was wrong. There *was* something wrong. The accident had caused some bleeding in Daniel's brain. It had damaged the part of his brain that controlled his sense of smell. The result was that Daniel had almost completely lost his ability to smell things. Because the sense of taste depends very much on smell, all he had now were three basic tastes: salt, sweet and bitter. He couldn't taste anything else. He could still enjoy the colour and feel of food, but none of it would taste of anything more than those three basic tastes, no matter what the food or drink was. That's what the doctor told him.

But, apart from that, he was fine.

'Of course I'm fine! Now can I go home?' he asked, impatiently. The doctor told him he could and that was what he did.

But this time he went home on the bus.

The first thing he did when he got home was book a table at his favourite French restaurant. He did not believe for one moment that his famous nose and tongue were no longer as sensitive as they used to be. It had only been a minor accident. No, a good meal, a glass of good wine and he would soon be back to his old ways. As for hospital food, well . . . everybody knows what *that* is like: it *always* tastes disgusting. In fact, cardboard would be an improvement on that awful rubbish.

After a bath and a shave he was all ready. He put on his favourite clothes, including his spotted tie and red jacket. He was looking forward to his meal. As always before eating out, he drank nothing stronger than water – he did not want any other tastes to spoil the sensitivity of his tongue. He had also arranged to meet Justin, his immediate boss and one of Happimart's chief marketing managers. Justin had left a message on his answerphone. He wanted to know if the Bordeaux business with old Colbert had been successful. Well, he would tell him the good news over a delicious meal.

*   *   *

They had the best table, the one overlooking the river.

Daniel recommended the veal with truffles and new potatoes in garlic butter. But first they must have Henri's famous onion soup. Henri was the best maker of soups in the business. The restaurant had brought him all the way from Provence in France just to make soups for them.

When the soup arrived, he waited for Justin to taste first. They had both turned down an aperitif and had drunk only mineral water to begin with. They had their wine glasses filled with wine from Burgundy, but they would only drink it *after* the soup – they didn't want to spoil it.

Justin tasted. He was a tall man of about thirty-five, with neat blond hair and a body which had once been fit but had got fatter with lots of good food. He wore an expensive suit and had the look of a man who was used to getting his own way. He was almost as fond of good food and wine as Daniel. In fact, it had been Justin's idea to produce *Dinner Party* for television with Daniel as one of its stars.

'Daniel, my dear boy, this soup is fantastic! Henri has never made better!'

Daniel smiled. Good old Henri! He took a spoonful of soup and put it into his mouth. He waited a moment for the heat of the soup to go down a little, while his tongue took in the flavour.

Salt!

All he could taste was salt! It tasted so terrible that he nearly spat out the soup.

Justin noticed.

'Daniel – whatever is the matter? Are you all right?'

Justin, he observed, had already swallowed two spoonfuls of the soup. Justin's taste was almost as expert as Daniel's, yet he had liked it. Could those doctors have been right? Had he really lost his famous sense of taste?

These thoughts flashed through his mind in an instant. This was hardly the time to admit anything about the loss of his sense of taste – not to a man who was going to give him a job that depended on it! He would have to pretend nothing was the matter. After all, Henri's soup could always be depended on – it was always excellent.

'Er . . . nothing,' he told Justin. 'Just a little something in the throat. This soup is delicious; do finish it.'

Justin smiled and finished his soup. He then praised the Burgundy, a wine that was a particular favourite of Daniel's, though tonight it tasted like warm vinegar as far as he could tell. In fact, it tasted so horrible that he had to try very hard not to spit it out. But he drank it.

They talked as they ate and Daniel told Justin about old Colbert's wine. Justin seemed delighted and was looking forward to tasting it. He asked Daniel to bring some to the Happimart office the next day for a tasting of some of the new wines Happimart had recently bought. Justin liked to try all the new wines before they went on sale, and it was a good way for Happimart's wine tasters to practise. Justin also knew that Daniel loved to show off in front of the other tasters. It was expected.

'Why, of course,' Daniel answered. But he was beginning to be afraid. The veal which Justin was now finding so tasty was just a salty piece of soft stuff in his mouth. He might just as well be eating the insides of a cushion. But he dare not tell Justin. The thought of attempting a wine tasting – an occasion he would normally look forward to – now filled him with fear. He would need time to do something. He had to act quickly.

'But wouldn't it be better, Justin, if we had the wine tasting at a later date?' he suggested.

'Daniel, my boy, why ever would you want to do that? Don't you want to show off your abilities to your *employers*!' The way Justin emphasised the word *employers* sounded almost threatening. Justin was not used to his arrangements being disturbed. If Daniel had a reason to change his plans it had better be good.

Daniel had to think quickly. He knew that Justin wouldn't want him on his television show if he knew about his problem; he might even find a reason to make him leave Happimart completely!

An idea formed in Daniel's mind, a desperate one but it came out of his mouth before he could stop it.

'Er . . . to give us time to bring over our new employee, Monsieur Colbert,' said Daniel. 'Old Colbert makes some of the best wines in the world; perhaps he would be a good man to test out *our* wines, as well as myself. After all, if he is to supervise our new vineyard it would be a good idea to get his expert advice on other wines, wouldn't it?'

Justin sensed that something was not right but didn't know what it was. He didn't really like Daniel but had always respected his abilities as a wine taster, even if he thought Daniel was greedy, with too high an opinion of himself. But, of course, if he wasn't able to do the job any more then there was no reason to keep him on.

'Why, Daniel, I never thought I'd hear you tell me that you valued somebody else's opinion above your own! You must be losing your abilities!'

'Not at all!' Daniel thought that old Colbert was sure to have a good nose for wines – in his business he had to have. He could simply agree with everything Colbert said. That would stop people finding out about him and save him from a huge embarrassment. He could pretend there was nothing wrong with him and just judge wines on their colour and feel – you could tell a lot about wines that way if you knew what to look for, as he did. Yes, he could use old Colbert to get him out of this mess until his sense of taste got back to normal. But that would be soon, he was sure.

'All right, Daniel. I'll leave the arrangements to you. Bring him over, fix a date and I'll get the wines. But Daniel?'

'Yes, Justin . . . ?'

'Don't make a habit of this. OK?'

*　　*　　*

Daniel went to see the doctor again. He had been certain that his condition was just temporary but now he wasn't so sure. Would he ever get his sense of smell and taste back to normal? He had to know – his future career depended on it.

'There's no way of knowing, Mr Appleby,' said the doctor. 'In most cases I'd say no, but your brain suffered very little damage. It might recover, but I can't be sure. I'm sorry I can't be more helpful than that.' That evening at home Daniel did something he very rarely did: he got drunk. He got drunk at home on brandy he could not taste.

The next morning he had a terrible headache and he stayed at home.

Daniel Appleby had to face the fact that his future now depended on Colbert. He didn't like the idea, but maybe he could use him. After all, he had saved his vineyard for him; it would go on making his beautiful wines. The fact that the old vineyard was now owned by Happimart and the old man was now just an employee wasn't important.

At least, Daniel didn't think so. And if he could get the old man to help him, nobody need know about his loss of taste. 'Surely,' thought Daniel, 'old Colbert could understand the pride we wine tasters have in our profession? After all, he's a proud man himself, in his way.' Daniel guessed that Colbert – like most wine experts – would love to try what other wines were on offer. In any case, he knew that Colbert would be needed to instruct Happimart specialists on the methods he used to produce his wine.

Daniel decided to risk it; he would tell Colbert everything about his accident and his loss of taste. Besides, Colbert owed him a favour, didn't he? But, just to be sure, he would tell him that he would get him sacked from his new job if he didn't help. He couldn't refuse then. He would get on the telephone and speak to him right away.

No problem.

The next few days saw Daniel Appleby busily making arrangements over the telephone with old Colbert, who agreed to be there in two weeks.

Thank goodness!

*   *   *

A week later Daniel got a phone call from Justin. He had just tasted some of old Colbert's wine and he was very excited about it.

'Daniel, my boy, I knew it must be good because of what you said but I never realised it would be *this* good. Once we start producing this we'll create a whole new market for quality wine – everybody will want it! And you must get Monsieur Colbert to bring any more of these wonderful wines he may have – the man is simply brilliant! You *are* a clever old thing, Daniel! But then you are the best in the business – Happimart is lucky to have you! I *am* looking forward to meeting Monsieur Colbert next week! I've invited people from the television company, photographers from the best newspapers – everybody! Don't disappoint me, Daniel because this is going to be big!'

Daniel was glad to hear Justin praising him again but he had not got back his senses of taste or smell. He had had to pretend that he still had his famous 'nose' for wine, whereas he had actually been depending on his eyes and his experience in order to do his job. It hadn't been easy. Old Colbert was going to arrive soon, and he realised that he really would need the old man for the wine-tasting.

He was not happy about that.

*   *   *

Old Colbert was not used to dressing up in suits. He felt uncomfortable in a tie. He would much rather be in his old shirt, looking after his vineyard – he couldn't help thinking of it as still being *his* vineyard, though he knew it was no longer. Instead, here he was at the Happimart offices in London, being introduced to a room full of men like Daniel Appleby. And there was Appleby himself, wearing his ridiculous red jacket, smiling and holding a corkscrew. He was busy telling everybody all about 'Monsieur Colbert's marvellous wines' and how lucky he had been to be the man who had discovered them.

Appleby had told Colbert he owed him a favour and Colbert was not a man who forgot to pay back what he owed. Not at all.

Justin was smiling as he stood by the table full of empty wine glasses. He tapped a glass on the table with a spoon. It was surprisingly loud. Everybody turned around to look.

'Gentlemen,' he said, 'Monsieur Colbert has kindly agreed to bring along some more of his wonderful wines for us to taste today. This promises to be a treat indeed! Daniel, if you would be so kind . . . ?'

Daniel turned to Colbert who then handed Daniel one of the bottles he had brought with him. 'This is one we made recently, Monsieur,' said Colbert. 'Shall we taste it first?'

Daniel smiled as he pulled out the cork and poured out a measure for the old man.

Justin had insisted that Daniel take charge of the wine tasting – it was his way of saying he trusted him. Fine – that suited Daniel. Now he could make sure that the wine was completely under his control. Just as he wanted. The photographers were all taking pictures and television cameras were pointing at him.

Good. He was enjoying himself.

Colbert lifted up his glass, smelled the liquid first, tasted it, then spat it from his mouth into a small metal bucket kept on the table at such occasions. He looked at Daniel and gave a little nod, barely noticeable to anybody else. That was the signal he had arranged with Colbert.

Now he could start showing off.

'My friends, Monsieur Colbert has been good enough to allow me to be the first to taste the latest wine from the Colbert vineyard.' Daniel paused to pour out a measure into his own glass from the newly opened bottle. 'If you would allow me . . .'

Daniel did what everybody had come to expect of him: he smelled the glass with his expert nose, breathed deeply, then took a mouthful of the deep red liquid, taking care to roll it carefully around his mouth before spitting it into a bucket.

Everybody waited while he looked upwards, as he always did before giving his judgement on a wine. Finally, he spoke.

'This wine is truly a fine example of a great wine, full of fruit and with excellent body. It is, to wine, what a Picasso painting is to art – a true masterpiece. One cannot taste a wine like this and not feel that one has tasted greatness. Monsieur Colbert – you have made a wine fit for the gods!'

'Well!' said Justin. 'Let's not waste time, gentleman. Your glasses, please.'

He poured some into everybody's glass before raising his own.

'Let's drink,' he said, 'to Monsieur Colbert, his great wines and the man who discovered them for Happimart – Daniel Appleby!'

Daniel felt proud as he saw everybody's glasses raised. Proud and glad that it was all over.

All of a sudden there was a rush to the wine buckets and the sound of loud coughing. Everybody spat out the contents of their glasses with a look of disgust on their faces.

'Vinegar!' said Justin. 'Red wine vinegar!'

'*Oui*, Monsieur,' said Colbert. 'Our latest – the best vinegar made from only the finest red wine, fit for the Emperor Napoleon himself, don't you think?'

And so it was: the best quality red wine vinegar one could find anywhere.

Justin turned to Daniel and stared at him. Justin looked very angry as the specially invited photographers took their pictures.

Daniel's face turned pale as he felt his career break into pieces like a glass that has been dropped on a hard floor. The other wine tasters didn't know where to look, though some of them began to laugh.

But none laughed as loudly as Monsieur Colbert, whose laughter filled Appleby's ears for the rest of his life.

A Nose for a Story

'Are you OK Miss?' asked the taxi driver. He could see in his mirror that the American lady sitting in the back seat, was having a hard time keeping down her expensive lunch.

'No, I am not! What is that *awful* smell?' the woman asked.

The taxi driver smiled to himself. He often had to explain the smell to wealthy foreigners after he had driven them a kilometre or so away from their hotel. It was not something their sensitive city noses were used to.

'It's just the sewage, Miss. The pipes from the toilets are old and the weather is hot in India,' he explained. 'There are many people in Bombay – the pipes get very full.'

The taxi driver almost felt sorry for his passenger. She was middle-aged but had a pretty face and shiny dark hair, though her teeth were too big for his taste. Yet he could see as he closed the windows and switched on the air-conditioning that many men would find her attractive. But he had long since learned to distance himself from the delights of his lady passengers. He thought of himself as a professional, like a doctor. He was above such things.

'Don't worry, Miss; there are no more big sewage pipes in the village where we are going,' he added, helpfully.

'Thank God for that!' said the woman, who was now beginning to wish she had not asked for the windows to be left open in the first place.

'No, they use cesspits – big holes in the ground where they put all their –'

'Thank you, driver,' the woman said quickly. 'There's no need to go into details. I can imagine.'

Desiree Malpen, in fact, had one of the best imaginations in her business. She was a senior journalist for the *National Diary*, a publication which was proud of being America's 'number one magazine for lovers of the truth'. Other journalists who wrote for more serious newspapers disagreed. They said that the *National Diary* loved scandal and dirt and didn't care how much it changed the truth in its stories. The journalists were right. Lots of pictures and lots of scandal – that was the *National Diary*'s recipe for success – and Desiree was one of the magazine's top writers.

The taxi drove on a long way outside the city until the road became rougher. Finally it stopped by a small group of houses off the side of the road.

'This is the place, Miss. It's the house to the left,' said the driver. He pointed to a house that was slightly larger than the rest and still had some white paint on its walls.

'But it's so small!' Desiree said in surprise.

'Best house in the village, Miss. The family has been there many, many years,' said the driver with some pride, as if he knew the famous writer who had lived there, though he had never met her in his life.

This was the house of the late Nyree Singh, the former society beauty and writer, whose highly praised novels had been made into several films and who had won the Nobel Prize – or was it the Pulitzer? Desiree wasn't sure. She had never read any of her books. She knew, however, that

Nyree Singh had been killed two months ago in a car crash just outside Bombay. Some people said she had been driving to the house of an Indian film star – a *married* film star. Desiree felt sure that the crash had been no accident. It wouldn't be the first time that such 'accidents' had been arranged. Perhaps there was a jealous wife involved . . . or maybe an angry relative who could not stand the scandal or embarrassment to the family name? She had a nose for a story and when Desiree Malpen smelled a story there would be a story.

And if there were no facts behind the story she would think of some.

She looked at the window of the house. A figure was moving. There was somebody still living in Nyree Singh's house. But who?

Desiree took a few close-up pictures of the house – she always liked to take her own photographs. They gave a personal touch to her stories and made her some extra money.

'That's fine. Take me back to the hotel now, driver. I'll come back sometime and take a closer look. And driver . . .'

'Yes, Miss?'

'Next time I ask you to open the windows for some fresh air, don't!' Desiree said decisively.

*   *   *

While Desiree was going back to her hotel in the taxi, Gopal Singh was looking at the old brown photograph of his younger sister, Nyree. It sat on the table next to the sweet-smelling flowers he replaced daily. She looked as he would always remember her – a beautiful young woman whose intelligence shone far beyond her own country. She was only forty-five when she died in that car accident, still beautiful and with so much still to give. She had been respected by artists and politicians all over the world. Yes, he was proud of his sister.

But she used to get so angry!

He laughed. It was easier to laugh now. Oh, the times they had argued over the company she sometimes kept. Gopal had not always liked the people she mixed with. Still, they had always been there for each other. Neither of them had married. She was married to her work. He had always looked after her, though he would never have admitted it to his proud brilliant sister who, in many ways, had been a child still. She was too idealistic, only interested in those who shared her ideals. She would argue her opinions with anybody, but her beauty sometimes attracted lovers as well as thinkers. She could not be trusted to look after herself and who else was there? They were the only ones left of their family. Only he had known Nyree: only he had understood her ways, her needs – perhaps more than she did herself.

And now she was gone.

People seemed to want her even more since her death. But it was still Gopal who looked after her memory and her work. He kept away all the journalists and other people who wanted a part of his sister to take away with them. She had given them her work, her wonderful books. Why should they want the part of her that was left to him, the part that was his sister? She had put her life into her work. Wasn't that enough for them?

Gopal had always been there for her. Even when she had mixed with the most famous people in India, she had always come back to her faithful brother and their peaceful little home in the village. Always.

Now there was a growing number of curious eyes, cars that stopped and looked, tapping on the windows, notes through the door. What did they want? Didn't they know she was dead?

But he would stay. He would end his days in the house that held his memories wrapped in the sweet smell of flowers.

What else could he want?

*   *   *

The *Excelsior* hotel was famous for its quality and luxury. It was *the* place to stay at if you were at all important or wanted to be thought of as being important. It was always full of foreign journalists. Whenever they were working in Bombay, foreign journalists always chose the *Excelsior*. Its attraction to journalists was obvious: it was a good place for both valuable information and scandal. Who knows what famous guests might say after too much wine at dinner? And there were always keen listening ears to catch every foolish word or careless whisper. This would later be served up to the world as a tasty dish of scandal in magazines like the *National Diary*. There were always plenty of readers hungry for details of the lives of famous people, especially if those details were interesting and personal.

That was why Desiree Malpen was staying there.

*   *   *

That evening at the hotel, Desiree sat at her table in the lounge looking at the setting sun through the windows. She was pleased with herself. She kept a glass of white wine with her but drank very little of it. This was what she always did. It meant that she could refuse offers of drinks from interested men while keeping a clear head herself. She was very good at listening to people who first drank too much and then said too much. On the few occasions when the conversation went from the boring to the exciting, she could reach into her handbag and switch on her tiny tape recorder – a very useful machine indeed.

Desiree was there to interview one of India's top film directors, Raj Patel. He was about to make a film based on *Indian Summer*, Nyree Singh's last novel. The Indian film industry, centred in Bombay, was becoming popular in the West, where it was sometimes known as 'Bollywood'. Desiree had no interest at all in Indian films or their directors, but her boss had told her that she might find out more about Nyree Singh and her film star lover. If anybody knew him, Patel did.

She recognised Patel coming towards her. He was quite old, well over sixty – Desiree preferred younger men – and was dressed in an expensive white suit. He was smiling and holding a gin and tonic. Desiree knew that older men were attracted to her. It was useful, though it could be risky if she stayed too long and they became too interested. She could see already that Patel's eyes were attracted by the necklace that sat above the low neckline of her dress. But she could handle herself all right. This guy would be no problem, she could tell. Patel came up to her and smiled.

'Miss Malpen, if I'm not mistaken . . . ?'

Desiree held out her hand as she welcomed him. She was expecting a handshake but Patel took it and gave it a kiss instead. It felt wet.

'They didn't tell me you were so handsome, Mr Patel!'

'You know how to please an old man, Miss Malpen,' Patel said as he laughed. 'But I was surprised when your magazine said it was interested in my latest film production. In fact, I'm pleased that the West is finally taking an interest in Indian cinema.'

'The whole world knows that you beat Hollywood in getting the rights to film Nyree Singh's last novel, *Indian Summer*. Naturally, everybody wants to know about it, especially since Nyree Singh's death,' said Desiree as she switched on her tape recorder.

'Well, I've always wanted to film Nyree's novels. I think it's best that her work should be filmed by Indians in India.'

'I hear that Nyree had quite an interest in Indian films . .. . and in film stars. Is that right, Mr Patel?'

And so the conversation went on. Raj Patel wanted to talk about his new film but Desiree wanted to talk about Nyree Singh and kept trying to get him to give away details of her involvement with one of his stars. Throughout it all, Patel simply smiled, drank his gin and tonic and kept trying to return to the subject of his film. But Desiree was determined and the subject always went back to Nyree's personal life. Finally he stood up.

'Will you excuse me for a few moments, Miss Malpen? I won't be long.' He had a phone call to make that he didn't want her to know about. And he left.

Desiree waited and sipped her wine. She was annoyed

that the old fool hadn't told her about anything apart from his boring film. He was back half an hour later. He seemed to be a little drunk. Desiree tried not to appear annoyed.

'Ah, yes, Miss Malpen – you were interested in Nyree Singh.' Patel's voice was louder than before and not as clear. 'And who can blame you? By the way, that is a most beautiful necklace you are wearing, my dear.'

'You were saying about Nyree Singh . . .' Desiree reminded him.

'Ah yes, Nyree . . . She was a remarkable woman – a woman who could have told the world a lot about the famous people she knew. I knew her well.'

Desiree's eyes opened wider. Nyree Singh's secrecy and hatred of publicity had been well known. 'Really? And did she tell you about . . . her secrets?'

'Not at all.'

Desiree almost got very angry but decided that silence was the best approach. She was right.

'But,' he continued, leaning over towards Desiree, 'she once told me, as her friend, that she kept a diary. "If the world only knew the secrets that I have written in this diary" she said to me, "they would be shocked."'

'Shocked?' said Desiree.

Patel looked at her with a concerned expression. 'If that diary were shown to the world, I tell you, there would be scandal. Scandal! Some people would be in serious trouble, I tell you! It's a good job her brother keeps it safe, or there would be a lot of respectable public figures who would be . . .'

'She has a brother ?'

'Oh, yes. Her older brother, Gopal – her only relation.

He was like a father to her. Yes, he has all her things, including that diary. It's safe in his hands. He's just a lonely old man who lives for his memories of his sister. He'll probably get rid of it sooner or later.'

'Get *rid* of it?' thought Desiree. 'Not if I can help it!'

*   *   *

While Desiree was deep in conversation with Patel, Professor Cyril Whitelaw was enjoying a cool glass of iced lemon tea in his small but comfortable room at the *Excelsior*. He was celebrating his first day in India by reading *Indian Summer*, the last novel by Nyree Singh, for the sixth time. He would have to know her works in detail if he was to write a great book about this secretive author's life. His publishers were paying for everything and expected results.

He hoped to see the house where she had spent so many years of her life very soon. Who knows what he might find there? Perhaps – and this was his secret hope – he might find some unpublished writings! The thought made him shake with excitement.

Whitelaw put down *Indian Summer* and his lemon tea and got up from his chair. He then played one of his favourite games – looking in the mirror and imagining his face on the back cover of his important future book: *Nyree Singh – Secretive Star*, the book that would finally make his name as an expert on serious modern literature. The thin face that looked back at him was that of a man of late middle age, with pale red hair and glasses. Its skin was pink from the heat and was already showing the first signs of sunburn. It needed a shave.

He decided to clean himself up and dress for dinner. After that he would have a drink in the hotel lounge. 'You never know,' he thought, 'there might be someone out there who knew her!'

Twenty minutes later he walked into the lounge of the *Excelsior*, where nobody knew Professor Cyril Whitelaw.

At least, not yet.

* * *

'My dear Miss Malpen . . .' began Patel.

'Call me Desiree, please.'

'Of course . . . Desiree. May I please introduce my brightest star, my finest actor and leading man, Ravi Narayan. He's going to star in my new film – *Indian Summer*. I've always wanted to make a film of my favourite book by my dear friend Nyree Singh – and now I am.'

'You naughty man, Raj!' said Desiree, giving Patel a playful tap on the wrist. 'You didn't tell me we had another good-looking man in the hotel! Why, he's almost as handsome as you!'

Patel laughed. They all did. It was a game Desiree was good at playing with older men. But this other man was not a day over forty and yes, he *was* handsome. But where had she seen him before?

Ravi Narayan smiled with white film-star teeth and said how pleased he was to meet her. The voice was familiar, too. That was when Desiree remembered him. His handsome face had been the only thing that had kept her awake through viewings of Patel's boring films. Her editor had insisted she watch them as preparation for this interview. She was glad she had decided to put on her best perfume after all. Perhaps it had been worth it. Now there was another link with Nyree Singh – perhaps he had been her film star boyfriend!

'I thought that Hollywood was interested in filming that book, Raj. I don't mean to be rude but why are *you* making it and not them?' It was a fair question and Desiree was curious to know the answer.

'It's all thanks to Nyree's brother. He is responsible for all her books now. And he likes my films. He wants the film made in India by Indians. By *this* Indian!' Patel pointed to himself and laughed loudly. They all laughed.

Their conversation was being listened to by a very interested figure with pale red hair and glasses who was sitting by the bar not far away, unnoticed by them, busily writing in a notebook. It was Professor Whitelaw.

'Yes indeed. I've known him for years,' continued Patel. 'He's spent his life looking after his sister. He still lives in their old house in the village. Goodness knows, Nyree had enough money to buy a palace but she insisted on staying there. She said it kept her feet on the ground. But it was Gopal who did that, if you ask me. He is getting old now, though, and his health is getting worse but he won't move from the place,' said Patel.

'So *he* decides what happens to her books?' asked Desiree.

'Yes. There must be lots of unpublished stuff there. Including that diary I mentioned. I'd love to have a look but Gopal won't let anyone near – he's no fool,' said Patel as he gave her a knowing look.

'Neither am I,' thought Desiree, who was already

making plans to visit Gopal the next day. She was determined to get that diary one way or another.

'But there I go talking about an old man,' went on Patel, 'when you have handsome Ravi to entertain you. Did I mention he was to star in my next film?'

Handsome Ravi talked about himself for the next hour or two, long after Whitelaw was gone. It soon became clear that Ravi had never even met Nyree Singh. And he didn't seem to notice Desiree's necklace at all.

*   *   *

The next morning, Gopal Singh was looking at the rising sun from his bedroom window. He was glad he had agreed to let his old friend Raj film *Indian Summer*. Nyree had always said that foreigners should film her books because only they could see India with a fresh eye. He had always told her that was nonsense. They had argued about it but what, in the end, could he say? They were not his books and that was that. But now he was responsible. He would do what was best. At last.

The previous night, Raj had told him on the phone that a silly journalist from that awful *National Diary* magazine wanted to see him. Raj, as Gopal well knew, had always liked attractive women – his marriage never changed that – but even he knew trouble when he saw it. And Desiree Malpen was trouble. No doubt about that. She was not interested in Indian films. That was for sure. So Raj had, with Gopal's permission, made up a story about a diary full of scandals about important people. Raj had been a good actor in his youth so, while he was talking to Desiree, he had pretended to be drunk and to be talking too much – he was good at that kind of thing. And she had believed every word, just as he had expected her to!

Of course, Raj and Gopal both knew that Nyree had never kept a diary in her life. He remembered Gopal once telling him about Nyree's little box of secrets, so he had quickly thought of the plan. They had realised that the filming of *Indian Summer* would attract interest outside India and not all of it welcome. Desiree Malpen was a good example. Raj told Gopal he could either send her away or he could carry out the joke. If she was more interested in scandal than his films she should not get any pity. Gopal laughed and told him to go ahead.

Good old Raj!

*   *   *

Desiree had also got up early that morning. Ravi Narayan had proved to be as good a talker as she was a listener. Perhaps better. Old Patel had smiled as he allowed his star to talk and talk and talk. Her cassette had soon finished and she hadn't got another. She had hoped to catch more details about Nyree Singh and her diary. Oh yes, there had been a lot mentioned – famous names, important names from all over the place – when Ravi took a breath and allowed Patel to talk for a while. This had not been often enough to please her, but by then her interest had been awakened. She was sure there was a story – and a big one, too. And as for Nyree's death in that so-called car accident! Had it *really* been an accident? There the smell of scandal there, she just knew it!

She had phoned Nyree's brother and told him she

wanted to get out quickly to see him. She was sure that old Gopal, or whatever his name was, would be as helpful as Patel had been, especially if he was a lonely old man. How could he refuse an attractive woman like her?

The diary would be hers. She was sure of it. Even if she had to steal it.

She decided she would wear a yellow trouser suit that would allow her to move freely around the place – she wanted to have a good look around when she got there. She looked great in the trouser suit and her appearance usually helped her get what she wanted. That and lots of nice perfume, of course. One had to smell nice.

Five minutes later she was on her way in a taxi. She had all the windows closed.

*   *   *

Later that morning Gopal Singh went out to change the flowers for fresh ones from the garden. The house needed the sweet smell. It had not been joined to the sewage system – it was an old house and still had no modern pipes. Waste was collected every month from a cesspit some distance away in the large garden. The cesspit was about two metres wide and over one metre deep and by the end of the month – as it was now – it smelled awful. But he was used to it.

As he walked down the garden he saw a man approaching, a middle-aged European man with glasses and pale red hair.

'Mr Singh?' said the man. 'May I have a word with you? It's about your sister.'

Gopal was always polite to visitors – if he liked the look

of them. This man didn't look as if he meant any harm. He decided to speak with him.

Professor Whitelaw introduced himself and they were soon sitting in the house, drinking tea next to the new flowers. Whitelaw explained about his plans for a book about Nyree.

'It will be mostly about her work, you understand,' he said, rather nervously.

'Not about my sister's private life, I hope? Nyree was a very private person and I want that to be respected, even now,' Gopal said firmly.

'I would never mention anything without your permission, sir,' the professor said. 'This will be the kind of book students of serious literature will read, I assure you.'

Gopal felt happier when he heard this. Nyree had always attracted both students and teachers of literature. And there had to be a book sooner or later – it was bound to happen. When he heard Whitelaw tell him about his plans to write a book that would celebrate her work rather than the details of her private life, he knew that it would probably be the first of many.

Gopal also knew that he was getting older and might not be able to control the things that were written about Nyree. If he insisted on having a considerable degree of control over the finished book, he could make sure that what was written was the truth and not the rubbish that *some* would like to publish about her. Besides, Whitelaw seemed to be honest.

'And what kind of information about my sister are you looking for, Professor Whitelaw?' Gopal asked.

'I'm particularly interested in any unpublished work you might have – any notes, unfinished novels, letters . . . diaries, perhaps?'

Diaries! Gopal wondered if this was another of Raj's jokes. But Raj had made no mention of this man.

Then there was a knock at the door. Gopal opened it.

There was an attractive woman in a yellow trouser suit standing there. She was smiling and carried a handbag. He could smell her perfume. This must be the woman from the *National Diary*. Gopal smiled and let her in.

Desiree thought the old man was smiling for a different reason. 'He's attracted to me,' she thought to herself. 'I knew he would be!'

Gopal introduced Whitelaw and Desiree's heart sank when she saw him. She was not glad to hear of his plans for a book – he would be as interested in scandal as she was. Maybe she could take his mind off the diary. She put on her sweetest voice, but Whitelaw did not react as she had hoped. He didn't look once as she leaned over while reaching for some tea. She might just as well have been his mother. No luck there. At least the old man seemed to be giving her his attention.

She explained, still in her sweetest voice, why she was there. She said that she wanted to describe the human side of Nyree Singh in her magazine, the side that would show the world what a wonderful person they had lost. Was there anything that he could show her readers? Letters? A diary, perhaps?

Gopal smiled.

'Come, let us all walk together in the garden. Then we can talk,' he said.

Gopal picked up an old metal box from a table, the kind with a lid and a lock, and carried it with him. He led them past the flowers by his sister's photograph and out to the garden path. There was an unpleasant smell.

At first the smell was not too bad. Then, as they went on, it got stronger.

'My sister was a secretive woman,' said Gopal. 'She knew many important people, many famous people. But she never said anything about her private conversations with them to me or to anyone. She respected her friends – even her enemies – and would never repeat to anyone what they said to her.'

As they walked the smell became almost too much. Desiree's face was turning pale and Professor Whitelaw, too, was looking very uncomfortable. Gopal went on.

'This box contains the only real secrets my sister ever kept from me. I once promised her I would never open it and I never have, even though I have the key.' He stopped and looked at his two guests, who were both trying their best not to be sick.

'This cesspit, which you see in the ground in front of us, is to be emptied tomorrow. It contains the sewage from the past month . . .'

They could see it in front of them. It was almost full, and the smell rose from it like an evil ghost.

Then Gopal did an extraordinary thing: he threw the box into the cesspit. It went through the air and landed in the middle. Desiree and Whitelaw looked on helplessly while the box sank slowly to the bottom, leaving only a few bubbles in the brown liquid.

'If you really wish to know the secrets in that box, they are yours. I will be at the *Excelsior* this afternoon. In fact, my good friend Mr Raj Patel will be arriving to take me there at any moment. The person who brings me the box may collect the key from me in the lounge of the hotel at four o'clock this afternoon – just in time for tea. Goodbye for now, my friends. It was a delight meeting you both. Perhaps we shall meet again . . .'

And Gopal walked down the garden path and left them there. Their eyes went from him to the cesspit and then to each other. Both of them wanted the box and what was in it, and there it lay, separated from them by deep, bubbling brown sewage.

* * *

Raj Patel and Gopal sat drinking tea in the *Excelsior* lounge at three forty-five that afternoon. Music from a string quartet was playing. As they laughed together a third person came to join them.

It was Professor Whitelaw.

'I'm sorry, Mr Singh, but I just couldn't do it. Not for anything. I'm afraid I have rather a weak stomach. Still, I don't suppose anything in that box would have made much difference to a book about Miss Singh as a writer . . .'

Gopal smiled. 'Quite right. Think nothing of it, Professor Whitelaw. I hope you did not mind my little test of your . . . er . . . intentions! I can see you are a man with high standards. Now do sit down and join us for tea. Let me introduce you to my good friend, Mr Raj Patel; he is a very fine maker of Indian films.'

For the next ten minutes they all chatted about Whitelaw's ideas for his book, and Raj Patel's plans for *Indian Summer*, starring Ravi Narayan.

It was almost four o'clock when Desiree Malpen arrived with an old metal box in her hands. She was wearing a loose blue dress and smelled of strong perfume. But there was another smell mixed in with it, a bitter unpleasant smell which defeated all the efforts of the perfume to hide it. Her hair was still wet as though she had just come out of the shower. She smiled but it was an angry smile. She placed the box in the middle of the table, almost knocking over the vase of roses.

'Well, Mr Singh, here it is. I got it out. None of those taxi drivers would do it so I did it myself – ruined my clothes and had to pay for the damned taxi to be cleaned. God knows what they thought when I finally got back here! But here it is. Now are you going to open it?'

'Of course, my dear. At once,' said Gopal. He took a key from his pocket and didn't seem to mind that the box was not entirely clean. He turned the lock with a quick motion of his wrist and held the box out to her.

'Take it; it's yours.'

Desiree took the box and, looking very pleased with herself, opened it. She took out some old pieces of newspaper, which had gone brown and hard with age. She looked at them and stared at Gopal angrily.

'What on earth are these?'

Gopal Singh looked at the old papers.

'Cricket reports! We both loved cricket, but I hate reading results of matches I haven't seen – and Nyree loved collecting them. She was a sweet old thing, don't you think?'

Arlo's War

The snake's world was a silent one. Its world a box with a glass front. It was staring at its next meal. Its meal, a rat, was staring back.

The rat sat frozen with fear in the corner of the large box. It heard a soft shaking sound and answered with a few high sounds of terror. The snake was hungry and moved quickly. It was a big North American diamond-backed rattlesnake, almost two metres long with enough poison in its bite to kill several men. The rat was soon dead and the snake stretched its jaws to begin the business of swallowing its meal.

Arlo Penton sat and watched through the glass as Susie ate her rat. The sight made him feel a little uncomfortable – it always did – but that, he thought, was the way of Nature. And he did admire snakes. He admired their smooth beauty and their beautiful patterned skins. But most of all he admired their deafness.

Arlo had discovered some years before that snakes were completely deaf. They depended mostly on their highly developed sense of smell, and their tongues could actually *taste* smells from the air. As well as this, their expressionless eyes could see the heat given off by the bodies of other animals. Arlo watched with feelings of deep respect as the rat slowly disappeared down Susie's throat.

The snake lived in a world without annoying continuous noise. A silent world. To Arlo, snakes stood for beauty and perfection. He loved to watch them and admire them. If only his own world could be as silent as theirs! That was why he had caught Susie. More correctly, he had Chico – a local gardener – catch her for him. Susie had been caught in the rocky dry land that bordered Tucson, Arizona, where Arlo lived. Chico was most casual in the way he touched dangerous snakes. Sometimes he would even eat them. 'They're good to eat and they're free,' he would say. This disgusted Arlo, not because he didn't like the idea of snakes being used as food, but because he thought it failed to give the snake enough respect. Nevertheless, he was glad Chico had found Susie. She was a beauty.

Arlo liked living at the edge of town. He had to drive to work and it took him over an hour each way. It was noisy and hot, but at least he had quiet when he got home. Quiet was very important to Arlo. As a young man he had been a soldier and had fought in a war. His mind had been damaged by the noise of loud and terrible explosions and he had to be sent to a hospital at home to recover. He had met his wife, Maria, there. She was one of the nurses who had looked after him.

He still hated noise. 'Everybody talks about pollution,' Arlo would say to anybody who would listen. 'The way we poison our environment with this and that, yet the one thing which *really* poisons the quality of our lives is noise. Everywhere you go you hear people making noise, noise, noise. Where can you hear the birds sing these days? Not in the city, my friend. All you hear is traffic, loud radios and people with noisy machinery. Twenty-four hours a day it's noise, noise, noise. It's enough to drive you crazy.'

Too much noise took Arlo back, in his mind, to the war

with its loud explosions that had brought death and suffering. Maria had saved him from madness. Maria and his work and his pills.

To look at, Arlo was like many other fifty-nine-year-old men: he was of average height and his once-dark hair was now grey. He was neither fat nor thin and dressed casually – usually in black trousers, a blue shirt and his favourite cowboy hat. His thin face had taken on a more troubled look since Maria had died of cancer one year before. She had helped him through the bad times and made sure he took the pills he needed to keep him calm.

But now Maria was gone.

They had no children. Most of Arlo's time was now given to his work. Even when he was at home he would be thinking about work, putting new ideas down onto his computer. His work was his life.

Arlo had a job in a company called Teckno-Toys, which made electronic toys for children. He was the company's chief designer of radio-controlled toys, such as cars and aeroplanes. These toys were so clever and amazing that many fathers bought them at Christmas for their children, only to play with them themselves. The cries of 'Aw, Dad, can I have a go now?' were often heard in many homes where Dad had bought one of Arlo's marvellous toys.

His toys were indeed wonderful. The cars were tough but fast, while the aeroplanes were like magical birds that would fly up or down and turn in the air whenever you told them to. They could be guided from great distances with the powerful electronic controls that Arlo designed.

What Arlo liked best about his work was the electrical

side. He would leave the design of the toy's body to others, but design the electronic controls himself. By the time the toy was finished it would be the best that money could buy. Arlo had a garage full of small model planes, boats and cars he had made. He often used them to help test out new designs at home – that was why he had been allowed to keep them.

The Teckno-Toys factory was quite separate from the place where Arlo worked. He needed quiet so that he could concentrate and did not want loud upsetting noises to remind him of the war. He could never do this next to a noisy factory. He did his work in an old large house in the centre of the city called The Havens, which was owned by the company. The house was unusual in having its own spacious grounds that protected it from the loud noises of the city. Arlo worked there with a few other favoured employees. They would send their designs to the factory, which would build the models then return them to Arlo and his colleagues to be checked. This arrangement suited Arlo: he had a quiet place to work in, while Teckno-Toys got top-quality new toys that were sure to sell well. Keeping Arlo happy at The Havens had been worth it to them. So far.

Arlo had made enough money from his work to buy a spacious house outside the city and away from the noisy traffic. He built a large wooden tower in the garden so that he could control his models from great distances. He loved that. But he missed Maria and his sleep was sometimes troubled, especially when he forgot to take his pills. But, at least he had his work to take his mind off the war. Work was all he had left.

*   *   *

Bernie Dimaggio, Vice President of Teckno-Toys, held a towel as he watched his boss on her exercise cycle. She often spoke to him while doing her early morning exercises in the private gym she had next to her office. She got off the machine and he handed her the towel.

'He's not going to like it, Miss De Cruz. You know how he feels about the place!'

Bernie's suntan could not hide the way his face turned red as he spoke

'You seem to forget who you are talking to, Mr Dimaggio: *I* am now the head of Teckno-Toys. My father was old-fashioned in his ways. He made this company but if we are to become the market leader we must change with the times.'

'But Miss De Cruz . . .' began Bernie.

'Enough, Mr Dimaggio. You may be Vice President and your concern for one of our . . . er . . . senior employees is understandable. But we have a business to run. We have to progress; we have money to consider. We can't afford *not* to sell a valuable property like The Havens just because an old man close to retirement likes a bit of quiet, not when we need the money for building up the factory. It's just not good business sense, Mr Dimaggio, and we both know it.'

'But Arlo has been working at The Havens for twenty years! He couldn't work anywhere else now. You knew him when you were just a kid, Miss De Cruz . . .'

'I'm not a 'kid' any more, Mr Dimaggio, in case you haven't noticed. And I have a business to run. The property will be sold. If Mr Penton wants to continue to work for

Teckno-Toys, he will have to work at the factory, like the rest of us. Or he can go. I trust you will let him know of this development at the appropriate time.'

'You mean after he's completed the designs for the new season's models?'

'Exactly. No sense in upsetting him just now. Not while he's doing useful work. It's not good business, Mr Dimaggio, you ought to know that,' said Eva De Cruz firmly.

Bernie Dimaggio had been with the company since Eva De Cruz had been a child. He had seen the business grow as Eva grew. It was a successful business, though not yet the biggest of its kind. He looked at his new boss, the twenty-five-year-old daughter of Diego De Cruz, his former boss and friend. Eva had studied at the best business school and she wanted to show the world that she was going to be better than her father had ever been. Better and richer.

After Diego's wife, Eva's mother, had died fifteen years before, Diego De Cruz had put all of his energies into the business. The education of his daughter and only child was left to private boarding schools, where she had lived for most of the time. She had been educated from a distance, like one of Diego's toys.

And Eva was the result. Everything about her was businesslike, from her usual dark blue suit to her electronic organiser. Bernie sometimes wondered if her brain had become electronic, too.

And what would happen to Arlo once he was told about the sale of The Havens? Both he and Diego had been in the army with Arlo during the war and had become friends.

After the war they had given Arlo work he could do in peace. They wanted to help him put his broken mind back together. Diego had promised Arlo that there would always be a peaceful place for him to work at Teckno-Toys. What would this news do to him?

'Couldn't you find somewhere else quiet for him, Miss De Cruz,' Bernie asked, 'where he can carry on his work? Diego ... I mean, your father ... promised Arlo somewhere quiet a long time ago!'

'That was then, this is now. We can't afford to treat him any differently from the rest of us, Mr Dimaggio,' she said after drying her face with the towel and throwing it back to him. 'Now excuse me, but I have another appointment in twenty minutes.'

Eva left him with the damp towel. Bernie was close to retirement age himself. He felt sorry for Arlo. Diego would have done something to help, but not Eva. He might lose his own job if he didn't do as she told him.

Bernie felt older and weaker as he walked out of the gym.

*   *   *

While Eva and Bernie were talking, Arlo was getting into his car to go to work. He had forgotten to take his pill again. His face was already sweating. It was a bright sunny morning and the roads would be hot. He was glad he had completed the new designs and was looking forward to handing them in personally, as usual, to Bernie Dimaggio. They lay on the seat next to him as he drove to the city centre. The road was already busy with the morning rush of traffic.

Arlo had to stop at a set of traffic lights. The car next to him was a sports car with an open top. The man at the wheel was young and wore dark glasses. He was listening to loud rock music and was nodding his head to the rhythm as he listened. Arlo could not understand how anybody could listen to such a loud noise without damaging their ears. He could feel the noise hitting his own head in solid waves. It was painful. He shouted to the man to turn the sound down. The man saw him and laughed, then turned the sound up even more. Fortunately, the lights changed at that moment and they both drove away. Arlo let the sports car speed ahead, taking its noise with it.

Everything seemed to be noisy on that journey. Other cars had noisy radios. Arlo swore at the Tucson rock music radio station as he passed it by. Then he heard some loud machines at some new building works. Car horns sounded at every pause in the stream of traffic, and everywhere people seemed to be shouting, shouting, shouting.

At last, the turning for The Havens came into view. He could hardly wait to enter the peaceful building! As he drove through the private grounds all the awful noises disappeared into the distance. When Arlo stopped the car his body was shaking and covered in sweat. Echoes of loud noises were still in his head, some of them terrible memories of the war. He took a few deep breaths to calm himself, then picked up his designs and walked into the big house.

*   *   *

It was nine o'clock at The Havens. Bernie Dimaggio was early. He was waiting in the office as Arlo walked in. He noticed that Arlo was holding the envelope containing the new designs. He also noticed how upset Arlo looked.

'Hi Arlo! Hey, are you OK? You don't look so good, if you don't mind me saying so. Are you still sleeping OK? Hey, if you need anything just say the word.'

Arlo smiled. Bernie was always concerned about him when it was time to hand in his designs. Did he think he would finally go crazy before completing them? Probably. Bernie had always been a worrier. Arlo looked into the familiar suntanned face and answered, 'I'm fine, Bernie. At least, I would be if I walked around with my ears closed. I swear this town is getting noisier every day.'

'Oh no,' thought Bernie. 'I hope he's not going to give me another long talk about noise pollution!' Bernie decided to change the subject quickly.

'You have the designs I see, Arlo. All ready for production?'

Arlo handed over the envelope, giving it a firm tap with his hand on the way.

'You bet, Bernie. This one is going to be a winner, I'm telling you. The kids are going to love it! It's easy to control, yet it's as quiet as a baby asleep in its mother's arms!'

'Everything's checked?' asked Bernie.

'Checked and double-checked,' Arlo answered. 'You ought to know me by now.'

Bernie did know. If Arlo said something was ready, it was ready. He put the designs in his briefcase and began to walk towards the door as he thanked Arlo. Then he stopped and turned to him, pulling another smaller envelope from his jacket pocket.

50

'Oh, I almost forgot . . .' said Bernie, though he had done no such thing. 'Here's some mail from the factory for you.'

'What is it?' Arlo asked as he took the envelope.

Bernie looked at his watch. He wasn't brave enough to face Arlo's reaction to the sale of The Havens. 'Hey, I've got to go to a meeting right now. See you later, OK?'

'OK,' said Arlo as Bernie smiled nervously and left. 'He sure was in a rush,' he thought. 'Maybe the noise has been getting to that guy, too. I wouldn't be surprised. Nothing surprises me anymore.'

Arlo sat down with a sigh and opened the envelope.

*   *   *

Eva De Cruz tested her coffee. It was black with no sugar, just as she liked it. As she sat at her office desk she thought that things, on the whole, could be a lot worse. It had been a month since the old man had left them. She had expected him to make a lot more fuss about the whole business. She knew he would never work in the factory grounds, not with his unreasonable attitude towards perfectly normal noise levels. All the other designers had agreed to the new arrangements. She couldn't change the world just because one employee had had some unfortunate experiences in the war. That wasn't her problem. Besides, The Havens had been knocked down by the new owners. They had already started to build a new radio station on the grounds. It was going to be the biggest rock music radio station in Arizona. Teckno-Toys had made a lot of money out of the sale. And if the old man didn't like it . . . well, that was just too bad.

Eva De Cruz had known Arlo for most of her life. She

had even played with some of the toys he had designed while they were in the testing stage. She had loved the toys but the man who designed them was, to her, just a strange old man who hated noises. She had never been close to him, though she had liked his wife. Maria was nice. It was true that the old man had been a first class designer but nobody is so good that he can't be replaced – especially if they're half crazy and more trouble than they're worth. Besides, the company had already made a lot of money from his designs. There were plenty of excellent young designers already applying for his job – they weren't troubled by noise at all. They were cheaper, too.

'No, there will be no problem replacing Arlo Penton,' Eva thought to herself as she poured out a second cup of coffee. 'No problem at all.'

*   *   *

Arlo had given up his job as soon as he had read the letter. There was no way he was going to work in that noisy factory! He had enough money saved. He could take care of himself all right. He didn't need false friends who broke their promises. He could manage alone. That's what he kept telling himself.

But it was a month since he had left his job and the noises in Arlo's head were getting worse. He often forgot to take his pills now. Sometimes he would wake up in the early hours of the morning covered in sweat and screaming at the ceiling. Only now there was no Maria to help him get over the nightmare. His memories of the war had returned and he was alone in the middle of them. To Arlo, it seemed that the guns were firing again. The guns in his head and the sounds outside were joining together. The difference between memories and reality was breaking down in his mind. When he went out in the car for his groceries he would hear the guns. Every loud radio, every noisy machine seemed like an exploding bomb to his ears.

He wondered why something wasn't done about it but nothing ever was. And all the time the noise was there. Why didn't people notice what was going on? Were they all deaf? *He* could hear the enemy. His enemy was noise.

He had to do something or he would go crazy. Nobody else seemed to be doing a thing about it. It was all up to him. He would have to stop the noise.

But how?

*   *   *

'That ought to be enough,' said Arlo. It was one week later and he had decided what he would do. He had been making the tower he had next to his house higher and stronger so that he could increase the range of the radio signals to his models. He placed his electronic equipment on top of the tower and the higher he built it the better his electronic equipment worked. He now had more control over his wonderful models than ever before with a range that allowed him to fly them high over the city.

Arlo had a wide variety of models to choose from. He had, over the years, collected over a hundred models in his garage. They were all in perfect working order. Teckno-Toys had let him keep them. He had tiny television cameras fitted to his models. This allowed him to see on his computer screen indoors where his models were while they were in use, even when it was cloudy or too hot for him to go outside. Arlo had learned a lot about how to make explosives during the war. He could attach a small but powerful explosive onto a model and then, from the comfort of his own home, direct it to a target. The video cameras would show him exactly where his target was; all he had to do was aim the model (usually an aeroplane) towards the target and BOOM! – the target was destroyed.

Nobody suspected anything. Arlo, after all, was just working on his models like he always did. No-one knew that he was making bombs as well. Chico called by with more rats for Susie. He saw Arlo working in his garage where Susie lay sleeping in her glass-fronted box. Chico liked Arlo, even if he didn't eat snakes. He stopped to watch in admiration while Arlo flew one of his wonderful models high into the sky.

He had no idea that Arlo's campaign against the enemy had begun.

*   *   *

Arlo's first bombing campaign was against the old Tucson rock music radio station. It was successful. Just one small model aeroplane had delivered enough home-made explosives to bring down the radio station's tower. It was easy. They wouldn't be playing loud music from that station for some while.

Tucson's local papers all published stories about a strange explosion that had blown up essential equipment at the local rock radio station. Nobody had been hurt in the explosion, they said, but the station would be out of action for a long time. The police could see no motive for the crime but did not reject the idea of some individual playing around with explosives for fun. This was worrying.

They were right to be worried. Over the next week there were several more explosions: large noisy machines on building areas were destroyed and a fireworks factory was seriously damaged. But nobody had been hurt. Not yet.

*   *   *

It was a few days after the explosion in the fireworks factory and Sheriff Calhoun was in the office of the Vice President of Teckno-Toys. He badly wanted a cigarette. He was trying to give up again and had not brought any cigarettes with him. Worse still, none of the other officers smoked so he couldn't even get a cigarette from one of them. This was making him bad-tempered, but he had a job to do. He stuck another piece of chewing gum into his mouth.

'Tell me again, Mr Dimaggio . . .' The Sheriff paused as he softened the fresh gum in his mouth. 'You told me when you rang me on the telephone earlier that this guy – what was his name . . . ?'

'Arlo Penton, Sheriff.'

'Yeah, Arlo Penton. You said he had been one of the top designers at Teckno-Toys?'

'The best we had. That's him in that picture on the wall just there. He's the one holding the model Mustang fighter plane. That's our biggest selling model and he designed it.'

Sheriff Calhoun looked at the picture in Bernie Dimaggio's office. Bernie liked to keep photographs of all of Teckno-Toys' best toys with their designers. Arlo featured in a lot of them. In this one, Arlo was smiling and looked happy and relaxed.

'And you got rid of the guy?' asked the Sheriff.

'No, Sheriff. It was his choice. He . . . er . . . left the company a few months ago.'

The Sheriff recognised a note of guilt in Bernie's voice. Years of listening to countless interviews had trained his ears to know when somebody was trying to hide something. That was what he was hearing now.

'With less than a year to go before he was due to retire? He sure must have had a reason. Can you think of a reason, Mr Dimaggio? After all, you say you've known him a long time. Not that I'm accusing anybody of anything, you understand, but I have to ask these things.'

Bernie had felt bad about the way the promise he and Diego had made to Arlo had been broken. He felt bad about his own weakness before Diego's daughter – his boss – who had not respected that promise. He knew that Arlo must have been disturbed by the loss of The Havens but he hadn't been brave enough to talk to Arlo about it after he had given him the letter. Could Arlo have used his expert skills to make these explosions?

Bernie told the Sheriff everything about Arlo, about Teckno-Toys and The Havens and how he thought Arlo might be responsible for the explosions. Bernie felt glad to have finally told somebody how he really felt about things.

'So, what will happen to Arlo now?' Bernie asked.

'Now hold on, Mr Dimaggio. You may have given us a motive for Mr Penton, but we don't know that he did any of these things. There have been a number of explosions: at the Tucson radio station, some heavy machines blown up and the one a few nights ago at a fireworks factory. That caused serious damage. But we can't be sure that any one person is responsible for all of these crimes. For all we

56

know, there may be any number of people out there making their own bombs.'

'But you don't really think so, do you Sheriff?' Bernie asked.

Sheriff Calhoun took a few more thoughtful chews of his gum and wished he had a cigarette. He looked again at the photograph of Arlo.

Suddenly, he noticed a model aeroplane, like a child's toy, fly past and before he could reply, there was a loud BANG! from outside. Bernie rushed to his window to look.

'Sheriff, it's the factory. It's on fire!'

*   *   *

Arlo had been working hard. He could not see the results of his work immediately because the television cameras were destroyed once his models hit their targets. He had to listen to the radio for news of his work – not the loud music stations, of course. His last action had been against the electrical generator at the Teckno-Toys factory. Without the generator they would not have the power to work their loud machines, and the hated factory noise would be silenced at last.

Unfortunately, though the action had been a success, three people had been badly burned. He heard about them on the radio. It upset him. 'But it's not my fault,' he told himself. 'This is war. Every war hurts some innocent people. It's the enemy's fault, not mine. Once the enemy is defeated there will be peace. I have to fight on for peace. There's nobody else. I *have* to.'

But Arlo had no peace. His heart was saddened by the

news of the three injured people. And the noises that disturbed him had not been silenced. The enemy was strong and there was much work left to do.

He made his way to the garage again.

*   *   *

Arlo began working immediately. He had to do the next one right. He had no idea that the Sheriff and a large number of police officers were, while he was working, speeding towards his house in their cars. All he was concerned about was putting the finishing touches to his model Mustang fighter plane. He had saved the Mustang for the new radio tower they were building at the place where The Havens used to be. They would never finish it. No way. Not if he could help it.

It would not need much explosive, just enough to bring the tower down. That would be enough. He got his little computer ready as he switched on the video camera attached to the model aeroplane. It was time to fly.

Arlo placed the Mustang on the ground by his garage then sat down by his controls. He did not see the Sheriff's men, but they saw him. They had positioned themselves some distance away from him. They all had powerful guns. They saw the Mustang as it started to take off. A shot was fired before the model had gone far enough to leave the ground.

There was an explosion.

Arlo felt a force hit his ears and he was knocked to the floor. There was a pain in his arm. He had closed his eyes.

Was he dead? Had the enemy beaten him? He opened his eyes and saw that his arm had blood on it.

As he started to get himself up, Arlo did not see the pieces of broken glass on the floor behind him. He did not notice the angry shaking sound of the snake whose sleep had been disturbed. He hardly felt Susie's bite before he sank to the floor again. His eyes felt heavy as the daylight turned to darkness and death ran with the poison in his blood. But he was happy.

Arlo's world was, at last, a silent one.

Open Doors

Kathy Page had been blinded at birth.

She had been born two months early, and at that time doctors had not yet realised that giving a new baby pure oxygen to breathe would destroy the sensitive nerves at the back of its eyes.

But that was then. Kathy Page was now a leading journalist in British radio. She was best known for her intelligent, but tough, interviews of public figures and people in the news. A recent interview was typical of her style:

'So, your election promise to uncover political dishonesty, does that include the bribing of government ministers?'

'Of course. This government will not tolerate dishonesty of any sort.'

'Would that include the money *you* received from foreign businessmen and didn't tell your government about?'

'Er . . . that was a misunderstanding . . . I can explain everything.'

'Can you explain the government contracts given to those same businessmen shortly afterwards?'

'Well . . . er . . .'

'Thank you, Minister. And now over to the newsdesk.'

Kathy Page had no patience with any attempts to hide the truth.

She had a voice that was gentle and calm, almost motherly at times, which men found attractive. Nearly everybody she interviewed tended to relax more when she spoke. That was when Kathy was at her most effective. More than one politician had cause to be sorry for a careless reply to the relaxing manner of her voice.

Kathy knew better than most people how to listen to the human voice. She couldn't see all the little tricks people sometimes used with body language and the expressions on their faces to give false ideas of their real feelings. She could only hear what they said. It was almost impossible for the people she interviewed to hide the tiny changes of expression in their voices that showed what they really thought. No matter how hard they tried to cover it up, she could always tell when a person was feeling uncomfortable and could usually understand the reason why.

Kathy would be kind to guests who were not used to being the centre of attention. For example, she understood the natural shyness of an old lady who had been given a prize for her work with the poor. But if she thought a guest was lying she would not stop questioning until she had discovered the truth. If a lie had been told she always made sure her listeners knew it.

Politicians and businessmen often thought that somehow they could fool her. They rarely did. Kathy was too good at her job for that.

Her listeners loved her. She was their star. They knew that if anyone could find out the truth, it was Kathy Page.

Kathy had been in the business of radio reporting for thirty of her fifty years in the world. She was happy in her work. She had never married, though she was often told that she was attractive. She was. Her black hair was long and shiny without a touch of grey; her face was pretty without being weak, and the few lines which showed made it more interesting. Many hours of yoga had kept her figure in good shape. No, she was not short of male admirers. Occasionally she would allow one to take her to dinner if he could hold an interesting conversation, but she mostly preferred the company of her colleagues, her books and Trudy, her much loved six-year-old guide dog.

She loved music and the arts. She regularly went to the theatre for old, as well as new, productions. It was a favourite activity of hers. The only thing she ever regretted was that she could not see paintings. She had read a lot about great artists and their work and often wished that she could see a great painting, even if it were just for a short while. But then she would put away such thoughts; they were silly and senseless. It would never happen.

Television producers had often, over the years, tried to get Kathy to present her own chat show on television. They knew she was a favourite with the public, and they wanted to attract the large audience that such a show would surely bring. Kathy always turned them down. She felt at home with the radio. It didn't matter what you looked like; it was what you said that you would be judged by. That's what she always told everybody.

And besides, Kathy Page, the queen of radio interviews, was shy about her appearance.

* * *

'She turned you down? Again? Are you sure you told her just how much money we're offering?'

Mick Dean, the current favourite of his television company, waved his other arm around as he held the telephone. There was nobody else in the office but he waved anyway – it was just a way of showing his feelings. He couldn't understand how anybody could turn down an offer like this. He had had similar conversations before, all about Kathy Page.

'OK, but don't give up. Try again in a week. Yes . . . bye.'

Mick Dean put the telephone down. He was the company's youngest producer and was responsible for many of its newest and most successful shows. He was particularly good at producing chat shows and more 'serious' shows that interviewed people in the news. He believed that a lively argument was the best way to entertain viewers; it would make more people watch the next time. 'They like to see a good fight,' he would always say. 'And they like fighters.'

That was why he had always wanted Kathy Page to present one of his shows. 'Not only is she a good fighter, she looks great, too, and people respect her. She'd be a sure winner and I want her before anybody else gets her!'

Yet again his best man had failed to persuade Kathy to join him. But Mick Dean was not the kind to give up. He had not been the first producer to try to win Kathy Page over to television, but he was determined to be the last.

*   *   *

Kathy's radio show was one of the most popular shows on the station. She would interview people in the news and deal with serious issues. As well as the usual politicians and businessmen, she often spoke to artists, writers and scientists. The shows got more interesting for the listeners when Kathy questioned her guests, especially when the guests said things that Kathy found hard to believe. That really made things exciting.

It was getting towards the end of her morning show and her final guest was coming on. He was an American scientist, Dr Woodrow Percival, who was an expert in eye surgery. He interested Kathy because he had said that he could replace damaged eye nerves with tiny computer chips that would work just as well as real nerves, perhaps even better. Kathy took a personal interest in this. He had said, in fact, that he could make the blind see.

What's more, he had said that he could make *her* see.

Kathy had come across other 'experts' before. Sometimes they were more interested in getting publicity for themselves than in telling the truth, saying that a small discovery was greater than it really was. If this guy had any real doubts about his methods, Kathy thought, she would know it. It was wrong to raise the hopes of people who might otherwise have accepted their disability and got on with their lives. If he was offering false hope to people, he should be found out – and she was just the person to do it.

She introduced Dr Percival to her listeners and began.

'Dr Percival, you're going to give a talk later today about your new treatment. Could you, in simple language, explain how this treatment works?'

'Certainly.'

And that was exactly what he did. Kathy was waiting for any little changes in his voice that might suggest that he was not sure about what he was saying. His voice was calm.

It was not the voice of an old man – he was forty – but it had a quality that suggested strength of character. She questioned him at frequent intervals, listening carefully for any signs that might show his answers to be false. There were none. Everything Dr Percival said was said in a way that suggested he was being completely truthful. All of his answers were clear and open. Kathy could find no fault with the man's voice or his reasoning. Finally, she asked the question she knew all her listeners were waiting for.

'Dr Percival, you said that you could give *me* the means to see. That was a very personal thing to say. Were you being serious?'

Kathy listened. He had been good so far. If he was going to show weakness, it would surely be now.

'Miss Page, let me apologise . . .'

'This is it!' thought Kathy. 'He's going to weaken! He knows he can't seriously support the things he says he can do!'

' . . . for what the papers reported. They named you in particular when, in fact, I had only used you as an example. What I actually said was that people whose nerves had been damaged – in the way yours had, for example – could be helped by my treatment.'

But Kathy, though she heard no sign of doubt in his voice, wanted him to be very exact with his answer. She knew her listeners expected no less.

'Dr Percival, are you saying that you could make me see?'

'Well, I'd have to see your medical records in more detail, but I think so. Yes. Yes, I could.'

It was time for the end of the programme. Kathy

thanked her guests and the closing music was played. She felt excited, yet guilty, for feeling that way. She had always thought that even if she had been given the chance to see she would choose not to, not after a lifetime without sight. But at that time there had been no hope. There had been no point in hoping. Hope was like a door shut and with no key to open it. Ever.

But now, this doctor sounded sure of himself. She was certain of that.

For the first time since she was a girl she allowed herself the hope of sight. She found that she *did* want to see. She wanted to see those pictures in the museums, the faces of her friends, the sky at dawn and the stars at night. She realised she wanted it very much indeed.

Dr Woodrow Percival had to rush off to his talk. He thanked her and left.

Kathy heard the door of the studio close behind him. She knew that he might hold the key to doors that had been closed to her since birth. Could those doors really be opened for her? She knew she had to find out.

*   *   *

The newspapers the next day were full of headlines about the interview:

FAMOUS BLIND RADIO STAR PROMISED SIGHT BY AMERICAN EXPERT.

WILL THIS MAN GIVE KATHY PAGE HER SIGHT?

GO FOR IT, KATHY!

The readers and listeners loved it. Mick Dean loved it.

He immediately offered to pay all the costs involved if Kathy would work for his television company for just a few shows.

But Kathy hated all the publicity. She was not afraid to speak up for her listeners, but she hated the idea of strangers making unwanted investigations into her private life. And this, as far as she was concerned, was a very private matter indeed. She refused all interviews on the subject and turned down Mick Dean's offer straight away. She thought it was nobody's business but her own and that was final. No further mention was made of the subject on her show. Guests were asked not to raise the matter. They agreed, largely because they respected Kathy and could understand her situation.

But Kathy had been busy. She didn't want the world to know about her personal life, so she had arranged to meet Dr Woodrow Percival again in private. She met him at the house of her agent, away from her home and safe from the eyes of the public.

Kathy was a wealthy woman. She had made, over the years, a lot of money from her work. She could afford the cost of the operation in Dr Percival's hospital in California, USA.

Dr Percival was as calm as ever and was glad to help her. He drank his tea as he sat in an armchair, looking at Kathy as she fed Trudy a biscuit.

'I must repeat,' he said, 'that you'll be the first person to receive this treatment. It has worked in all the tests and all the computer trials. Having said that, I must also remind you of the risk involved . . .'

'I understand, Dr Percival,' Kathy answered quickly. 'I'm

willing to take that risk. This is something I've made up my mind about. If it works for me it will work for others. It'll be worth it.'

'Now don't misunderstand me, Miss Page; by risk I don't mean to your life – that risk is no more than it would be for any other operation. I mean the risk to your hopes. I *am* confident the operation will work but I'm not God. Nobody can say for certain that you will have the use of your eyes at the end of all this. All I can say is there is no reason I can see why the operation shouldn't be a success. Are you still sure you want to go through with it?'

Kathy took a deep breath then answered.

'Absolutely sure. When can you start?'

*   *   *

The operation took place one month later at the hospital in California. Dr Percival thought the operation went well. All that was needed now was a few weeks for the tiny computer parts to join with Kathy's sensitive damaged eye nerves. During that time Kathy would need to rest in bed with a bandage over her eyes. Her brain would be checked regularly. When it showed signs that the eye nerves were working they would take the bandages off.

In those few weeks Kathy had plenty of time to think about what she had done. There were moments of doubt, almost panic, when she asked herself if she had done the right thing. She thought she had long since put away the foolish hopes for sight she had once held as a girl. Yet here she was, hoping like a girl again. She felt afraid, yes, but also excited at the thought of entering a world that would be totally new to her, a world where she could see. It would be like being born a second time.

She wondered what colour would be like. Although it was a word she had often used and heard before, she had never *experienced* colour. She just could not imagine it, no matter how hard she tried. Kathy gave up trying and waited patiently for the day her bandages would be removed.

The day came.

Dr Percival decided that Kathy's brain signals were doing all that he had expected of them. Things looked very promising. It was time to see if the operation had been a success. He closed all the curtains in Kathy's room so that the light was low. He turned to her and spoke.

'Now, Kathy, we have to take things slowly. Even if things go well you won't have full eyesight to begin with. First of all, let's see if your eyes are recognising light. I'm going to take the bandage off and hold a light in front of your eyes. If you can see anything you won't need me to tell you – you'll know. But you won't see anything clearly yet, that will come later. Are you ready?'

Kathy nodded.

Dr Percival held a small light in front of her eyes as a nurse slowly and carefully removed her bandages. Kathy sat up with her eyes still closed. Slowly she opened them and stared at the light. Quickly, she turned her face away.

'Ow! What was that? It felt strange – there's something there, trying to get into my head!'

Dr Percival told the nurse to replace the bandages and then turned to Kathy.

'Kathy,' he said with obvious delight, 'that "something" is light! You've seen light for the first time! Congratulations – you can see!'

Kathy could tell from his voice that he was pleased. She felt confused.

'But . . . I thought there would be more to it than this . . . I mean . . . I mean . . . Oh, I don't know what I mean!'

'Don't worry, Kathy,' he said as he smiled. 'All you saw then was pure light. It will take a while for your eyes to get used to seeing colours and shapes. Your brain has a lot of sorting out of new information that it has never had to deal with before. It's bound to take a little while, even with the advanced training methods I've developed. The main thing is that you can see!'

'I can see!' said Kathy softly.

And underneath her bandages she was crying.

*   *   *

Over the next few weeks Kathy was progressively allowed to use her eyes more often. Soon she could tell dark from light, then she could recognise colours and shapes. But, for a while, she found it very difficult to deal with the huge amounts of extra information that her new sense was giving her every day. One of her most difficult problems was judging distance: she found it hard to tell the difference between near and far objects. She would reach out for things across the room as if they were near to her, or she would walk into close objects without realising how near they were.

But Dr Percival was patient. Kathy was taken on walks

around the hospital gardens, taken for drives in the car and shown videos and television programmes. Her eyes were gently exercised until they worked well.

'In fact, Kathy,' Dr Percival told her, 'your eyes are better than mine are. I need glasses and you don't!'

What Kathy enjoyed most was seeing the pleasing effects shapes and colours produced. She would see ordinary things as objects of great beauty – the black and white squares on a chess board, the shape of a hand, the colours of a flower. Sounds, for the first time in her life, took second place. Colours and shapes now filled her mind with pleasure beyond her powers to describe.

But most of all she was deeply fascinated by the changing expressions on the faces of people. She viewed every face she saw as a new world to explore, full of things to be discovered. Every smile, every frown was wonderful to her.

*   *   *

When Kathy finally left the hospital it was as if she were leaving home for the first time. She was nervous but excited and her heart felt light as she opened the door to leave.

Of course, all the newspapers were soon full of the story:

AMERICAN SURGEON GIVES SIGHT TO BLIND WOMAN

THE GIFT OF SIGHT!

KATHY PAGE CAN SEE! – Brilliant American doctor performs miracle operation!

Woodrow Percival had tried to keep things quiet, at least

until he was sure that Kathy had recovered fully from the operation, but he couldn't stop the news from spreading any more than he could stop the sun from rising. Soon he had film companies wanting to make a movie about him, publishers wanting his life story and a long line of newspapers and magazines wanting interviews. The scientific community wanted to honour him while businessmen saw many ways of marketing his ideas.

Dr Woodrow Percival's future was looking very bright indeed.

*　　*　　*

Kathy wanted to rest at home.

There was plenty for her to do there. For the first time in her life she could actually see her most valued possessions. Best of all, she could see her friends for the first time. And, of course, her dear dog Trudy, who had had to stay at home while she had been away.

Kathy discovered that the human face had a powerful effect on her feelings. It was as if there had been a great hunger in her life that had been so much a part of her that she had never questioned it. Not until now. She had never before realised what a smile looked like, and it often moved her to tears to see her friends smiling.

Then there was her taste in clothing. Before, she had always had to depend on the judgements of others to provide her with clothes that felt comfortable but looked smart. When she looked in her wardrobe she saw nothing but dark colours or pale things that looked like they had no colour at all.

'They've got to go!' she said, as she took some of the

clothes out and threw them onto the floor. She was determined that from now on she would only wear clothes that were in colours she liked. After all, she could now decide for herself what clothes she could wear!

She arranged to go shopping with Carla, her agent, the very next day. Trudy came, too. Kathy had still not fully learned how to judge distances very well, and Trudy was almost as useful to her now as she had been before.

Kathy enjoyed choosing her new clothes. She was surprised at how good she looked in them. It was a feeling she liked.

As Kathy was paying for them, Carla – who had a particular interest in fashion – said, 'Well, Kathy, you've certainly brightened up your wardrobe now! I like the new look; it suits you!'

Kathy had bought clothing that was food for her eyes. Her clothes had always been rather dull before – more than she had realised. These new clothes were colourful and cheerful. They made her feel happy.

Kathy found that she was watching a lot of television. She had never really bothered with it before. Now she watched it with deep interest. Quiz and game show presenters, and singers smiled all the time against a background of bright colours. Their smiles made them seem to be such lovely honest people, yet on the few occasions she had listened to such shows before her operation she had thought they sounded stupid and shallow. It was confusing but she was almost too happy to care. Almost.

Kathy discovered that she could now dream in colour and with pictures, too! Before this her dreams were made of sounds, voices and music. Now she could also see in her dreams and she was delighted. She took up photography and loved to see how pictures from life could be caught by the camera, like frozen pieces of memory.

The next thing to do was to go to a museum with Carla to see paintings by great artists, just as she had always wanted!

She could hardly wait. Kathy was used to getting up early – she loved the colours of the early morning – and she planned to visit as many London museums as she could during the day. By eight thirty in the morning she had had her breakfast and was dressed and ready to leave. The doorbell rang.

Kathy went to the door. She was expecting to see Carla. But it wasn't Carla; it was a young man who was smiling at her. He had a nice smile, she thought.

'Hello, Miss Page. We've met before. You may remember me from the television studios. My name is Mick Dean.'

*   *   *

Kathy had not been to a studio since before her operation. She had decided to take at least one year off work, no matter how the operation turned out. She had been thinking of writing a book about her life. It would be a challenge and she liked challenges.

But now she had a new challenge: Mick Dean had given her a television show of her own to present. He had wanted her to do it so much, he had told her, that he just had to talk to her himself. And that was exactly what he had done: he had just turned up at her door. It was totally unexpected. She probably would not have spoken to him otherwise. Kathy decided she liked him for it.

She had never really taken much notice of Mick Dean before. In fact, she remembered that he had sounded far too sure of himself for her liking. But she must have been mistaken. He had offered her her own show where she could interview people in the news. He had looked so honest and enthusiastic about it that she thought she really ought to give the show a chance. And he had such a nice smile. His teeth were lovely and white, apart from the shiny gold one at the side, which was rather attractive. And his eyes! She had never realised that eyes could be so . . . so colourful! His eyes were a lovely blue with a few fine little red lines around the white parts. Kathy decided she would do the show. Just one – to see what it was like.

*   *   *

Three months later the show was ready and about to start. Kathy had soon got used to all the things that went on in a television studio: all the lights, the people who were needed to make sure everything worked right and, of course, the excited studio audience waiting for the show to begin. Kathy was behind the scenes, wearing her new cheerful clothes and drinking a cup of tea. She was reading Braille notes with her fingertips – it was still quicker than trying to read written notes – about her first guest, an ageing actor called Archie Mason. He had written a book about his life in which he had told his readers all about his wives, his lovers and the famous actors he had known. He had given away a great many details about their private lives and the kinds of things they did. This had, of course, guaranteed big sales of his book. Kathy was sure that much of what he had written wasn't true and her aim in the interview was to make him admit it.

When the show began, Kathy was given a warm welcome. The audience was glad to see her back, though there were a few surprised looks at her colourful choice of dress. Archie Mason was introduced and he made his entrance. He was a man in late middle age, with dark hair, a moustache and dressed in a smart blue suit with a red tie and white shirt. He was still handsome and knew it as he smiled at the audience with his perfect white teeth, waving and showing an expensive gold watch on his wrist. He then turned his smile to Kathy as he gave her a kiss on the cheek before sitting down.

'He has a nice smile,' Kathy thought as she looked at his perfectly shaped teeth. She liked to see things that were bright and evenly shaped.

Kathy at once started to question Archie Mason about some of the more doubtful details of his book.

'I swear to you, Kathy, that nothing in my book is untrue. Honest,' said Archie as he smiled and showed his white teeth. Kathy's ears were hearing a voice that did not sound honest at all, but her eyes saw a big warm smile that looked open and truthful. Her brain listened to her ears but her heart looked at the smile. It was hard to believe that a man with a smile like that could ever lie. For the first time during a live interview she doubted her judgement. She decided to believe him.

From that moment on she was no longer sure of her own judgement. To the audience, it seemed as if Archie was the one in control, not Kathy. So long as he gave her a big smile he could say whatever he liked. Kathy simply nodded and said 'yes' and 'really?' to him. This was not what the audience expected. Where was the Kathy Page they knew? She should have known right away how to deal with a self-important old fool like this.

Her next guest was a politician who had broken some of his election promises. At least, everybody thought, she would sort *him* out; he was more like what she was used to. But the politician had been prepared well. He had a boyish look, though he was well over forty. But, most of all, he had a nice smile. She didn't know what to think of all the different signals she was getting from this man: his voice told her not to trust him while his smile told her he was honest. She could no longer trust her judgement. She felt confused. The politician said almost anything he wanted. Kathy knew she should have been asking more questions but she just didn't have the confidence in her abilities anymore. She was too slow and the politician was too quick.

After the show, Kathy knew she had done badly. She felt terrible. She was not surprised when she heard, not long afterwards, that her show would not be put on again.

She heard no more from Mick Dean.

*   *   *

Kathy finally found the time to write her autobiography. She began it soon after her appearance on television. It took her almost a year, but it became a huge success and made her a lot of money. Once again, she was in public demand. Because of her renewed popularity, she was asked by a different producer to make another television show. She turned down the offer. She didn't want to go through that again! Instead, she decided to return to radio and soon her old show was back.

Kathy wanted to show her fans that she was as good as ever. As her first guest, she chose the politician she had interviewed during her disastrous television show. Naturally, he expected an easy time of it again. He smiled as he looked at Kathy across the table. He didn't smile for long.

'Could you tell us, Minister, about your promise to reduce unemployment?' she asked him.

The minister began. 'Of course, Kathy, but you must realise these things take a long time . . .'

'Oh really? That's not what you said last month.'

She then went on to tear him apart, taking each of his promises in turn and showing how they had all been broken. He was, before a listening audience of millions, shown to be false and dishonest, just as she had first thought. This was what her listeners had been waiting for!

As the politician left, Kathy sat back and took off the black scarf she had tied around her head to cover her eyes throughout the interview.

Kathy Page – the queen of radio interviews and star of her listeners – was back!

.

A Gentle Touch

The touch of Mr Lo's needle felt gentle as a feather as it was stuck into Jamie's right ear. Jamie was surprised that he felt no pain, only a little itch. That wasn't too bad. He did not complain as two more needles were put into position. Then the same was done to his left ear. Jamie was left to relax for a while as the needles did their work. Mr Lo read a magazine and Jamie, though conscious of the needles hanging from his ears, sat in his chair and stared through the windows.

He saw bright sunlight, bright colours and streets lined with trees and many kinds of brilliant flowers. He could see tourists buying delicious snacks from street sellers. Shops displayed everything from pots and pans to paper toys, often outside where curious shoppers could see more easily. Everywhere he looked it seemed there were large paper signs in letters of red and gold advertising the latest festival. People were not dressed for the cold and wet, they were wearing light summer clothes and only wore hats to shade themselves from the sun.

Jamie thought about his life as it had been only two weeks before. He thought of the views he had then from his office windows: the grey winter skies, the wet crowded streets and the few miserable leafless trees which lined the streets of the London suburb he worked in. At five in the evening he would have been looking forward to the end of his working day at the small college where he had taught Business Studies for the last ten years. He would be lighting up his twentieth cigarette since breakfast and looking forward to another cup of strong coffee before he finally went back to his lonely apartment. He had been bored, bored, bored. His whole life had felt grey.

How completely different that was from the view which now met his eyes!

Jamie Russell was glad he had moved to Singapore.

He felt so good about it he had finally decided to give up smoking, with a little help from Mr Lo's acupuncture centre. He had always wanted to give up the harmful habit but had, somehow, always found a reason to continue, such as the stress of work or the end of yet another failed relationship with a girlfriend. This time it was serious. It would be in keeping with the fresh start he had made in his life as a lecturer in a respected Singapore college. New job, new life. And what better way to give up than through the use of the ancient art of acupuncture? After all, it has been used in the East for over a thousand years.

Acupuncture involves the use of fine needles placed into particular points on the body that are said to be the focus of important channels of life energy called *chi*. The needles then direct this *chi* into its proper place. It is said that many illnesses and bad habits are the result of *chi* being disturbed or blocked. Acupuncture tries to correct such disturbances and clear the blocked *chi*. That's what they say.

Ten minutes later, Mr Lo removed the needles from Jamie's ears. Jamie stood up and stretched his arms. He was not sure what his ears had to do with his smoking, but he was prepared to trust the expert advice of Mr Lo. Why shouldn't he?

'How do you feel now, Mr Russell?' asked Mr Lo. He was a short man who appeard to be about sixty, and he had to look up to speak to the tall figure of Jamie. 'Do you still want a cigarette?'

Jamie was disappointed to discover that he did want a cigarette, but he was too polite to say so. Instead he arranged for further treatment in three days' time. In the meantime, he had to take some horrible-looking powder and drink it in hot water at home.

'It will help to direct your *chi*,' Mr Lo promised him.

When Jamie got home and tasted it he nearly spat it out. It tasted like mud. But he was determined to finish it and finish it he did. Normally, his first reaction to unpleasant experiences was to have a smoke. To his surprise, he found he did not experience his usual automatic desire to reach out for a cigarette. He still wanted one, but he did not feel as if he would go crazy without one. He could manage.

Over the next three days at work in the college he smoked only four cigarettes instead of his usual packet a day. Even then he felt guilty about it. Normally he would feel like climbing up the walls if he did not have a smoke at least once every hour. Was the acupuncture treatment working? It seemed to be.

The next visit to Mr Lo repeated the treatment. The results were, as far as Jamie was concerned, marvellous. He felt no desire at all for a cigarette after the second visit. He took the awful-tasting powder, just to be safe, but the need for a smoke did not return. If anything, the thought of smoking a cigarette now made him feel quite sick.

The acupuncture had worked. In fact, it had worked so wonderfully well that Jamie wanted to find out more about it. What else could it do? If it could stop bad habits, could it also encourage good ones?

He decided to talk to Mr Lo.

*   *   *

Jamie's new job was going well. He liked his hard-working students and they seemed to like him. He found he was feeling more awake and full of life. He no longer minded all the marking of books and preparation of lessons and long meetings that had previously been so tiring for him.

He also started to notice how few local people actually smoked. Before then he had not really cared so long as *he* could have a cigarette. Now he began to understand just how unpleasant the smelly things were. That's how he thought of cigarettes now: as smelly things that were both anti-social and disgusting.

He was even avoiding the strong coffee he had previously thought to be essential. Alcohol, once a regular part of his life, had also been put away forever.

And it was all thanks to Mr Lo and his little needles.

Jamie visited the acupuncture clinic every week. He was beginning to look forward to the feel of the fine needles in his skin. He enjoyed waiting quietly in his chair while the marvellous needles did their work. He even enjoyed staring through the windows while he thought about his changing fortunes.

Jamie was getting to know Mr Lo quite well. He asked him about acupuncture and other Eastern treatments. He was surprised at the depth of Mr Lo's knowledge. Mr Lo had studied acupuncture for most of his long life. He was actually much older than Jamie had thought him to be – much older. Could this be because of his skills? Jamie wanted to know more. Perhaps he could be taught some of these skills. Then he would be able to use them on himself! Why not? He asked Mr Lo where he could learn acupuncture. To Jamie's delight, Mr Lo offered to teach him himself. The cost was very reasonable and Jamie was glad to accept. Lessons were arranged and Jamie made sure he attended them regularly.

He was an enthusiastic student.

* * *

Acupuncture had rid Jamie of many of his bad habits. He was beginning to think he would no longer have any bad habits to treat! After a while, Jamie felt sure he could start treating himself. Improving himself. He did not want Mr Lo to know about this in case he upset the old man. After all, he might see it as a sign of disrespect if Jamie stopped seeing him for his personal treatment. Besides, Mr Lo might not like it. He had ideas about acupuncture and other Eastern studies which, to Jamie's way of thinking, were old-fashioned.

One evening, during a lesson, Jamie asked Mr Lo what he could do to increase his ability to think, to become more intelligent.

'What do you want to do that for?' asked Mr Lo, much to Jamie's surprise.

'Well, I . . . er . . . I could do my work better,' said Jamie.

'You do your work well already, as far as I can tell,' Mr

Lo told him. 'And you already have a good brain; I can see that. The mind and the body should be in balance – why spoil it by overdeveloping a brain that is good already, eh? No, my friend, the *chi* is meant to be in balance in body and mind. Do not upset that balance. What happens when we lose our balance? We fall over!' And he laughed.

Jamie smiled. He liked Mr Lo. But Mr Lo was old with old ideas. And they were not ideas that Jamie shared.

*   *   *

Jamie Russell was thirty-four years old. He was still single, though he had not yet given up hope of meeting the 'right girl'. But there was no romance in his life. His job seemed, somehow, to take up all his time and energy. He had been unhealthy and unhappy. At least, that was how it used to be. Not any more.

Now, just one year after beginning his study of acupuncture, it seemed to Jamie that he felt fit and happy at last. He no longer smoked or drank alcohol. He had given up coffee. The only thing he did drink, apart from water, was tea. His body looked firm and fit, and his dark brown hair shone with health.

It was a pity about Mr Lo. Why did the old man get so angry about the progress he had been making? Jamie could not see anything wrong in wanting to improve himself, in making himself better – even superior. What was the problem? Things finally reached a crisis when Jamie said he wanted to use his *chi* to influence his students so that they would never forget what he told them. Mr Lo had refused to help him any more.

'You cannot do this foolish thing,' Mr Lo had said to

him. 'You must not disturb the natural way of the *chi* – it goes against all I have taught you. If you insist on this foolish action you will be my student no longer!'

It was clear to Jamie that Mr Lo, the master, was becoming jealous of his student. It was sad but perhaps it was for the best. Jamie stopped going to Mr Lo's lessons. He had learnt enough – enough, at least, to know that he had to find other ways of perfecting his skills.

The use of needles was not always practical. He couldn't use them at work or when he was travelling around. There were times when Jamie wanted to increase his *chi* so that he could give himself that extra rush of energy he often wanted. He could hardly produce a set of needles and start sticking them into himself while he was at work or on the bus. No, acupuncture did not have all the answers he wanted. But, perhaps, acupressure might.

Acupressure doesn't need needles. Instead it uses either special sticks or – even easier – the fingers to apply pressure to points of *chi* in the body. The principles are exactly the same as acupuncture so Jamie did not feel that he had to start from the beginning again. He was confident that he could learn this new skill quickly. He did not feel the need for a teacher this time. He would teach himself. Why not?

So he did. He got out all the books he could find on acupressure and studied them. He looked things up on the internet. Soon he knew how to apply acupressure quickly and successfully without attracting attention to himself. This was impossible if needles were used.

Jamie soon found he could do all the work he needed to do at the college in a quarter of the time he used to take. He also had at least ten times more energy than he had had before. There was lots of energy left over for his own studies, for his own improvement. Lots.

People were beginning to talk about him. His amazing ability to work hard and never get tired was frequently mentioned. These comments were never unkind and he remained popular with both staff and students, though he was well-known for expecting more work from his students than other members of staff. There had even been a few students leaving the course because they could not take the stress of the work. This was a pity but, after all, standards had to be kept up.

His interest in Eastern matters was no secret, though Jamie did not deliberately draw attention to it. His colleagues admired a man who was enthusiastic about his work, and they liked the fact that a Westerner showed such an interest in Eastern culture.

Jamie was becoming quite well known as somebody who knew about such things. Students would ask him for advice instead of going to their local experts. Jamie never asked for money. Once, after he had successfully treated a student's headache with acupressure, he was called to see the head of the college. He was told, kindly but firmly, that he was to leave treatments to those who had licences to do such things.

Jamie made sure he never made that mistake again.

*   *   *

It was soon after this that Adrian Tong, the Physics lecturer, asked Jamie if he was interested in the art of *Tai Chi*. Adrian was a friendly man, about the same age as Jamie, who always dressed smartly. He was a popular member of the college staff, known for his helpful nature. He mentioned it to Jamie as they were preparing to go home.

Jamie was interested. He had heard of *Tai Chi*, which was made up of slow elegant exercises that developed the *chi* and made it stronger. Every morning in the park he saw people of all ages performing the exercises, gently moving their arms and legs like trees in a soft wind. Amongst them was a pretty young woman who Jamie thought was very elegant indeed.

Yes, it did look like a good way to relax.

'My uncle is considered to be a master of this art,' Adrian told him. 'I am sure he would welcome such a keen student as yourself.'

And so Jamie became a student of Master Tong.

Master Tong was a slim young-looking man though he was over sixty years old. He was amazed by Jamie's knowledge of Eastern culture and agreed to teach him, though he would have to take his place with the rest of his students, all seventy-three of them, in the park at dawn each day. That suited Jamie. It would be a good start to the day.

The first lesson began the very next morning.

The park was next to the local shops. Many items were delivered to the shops at the start of the day and the roads were already busy with small lorries delivering vegetables, newspapers and all kinds of things needed for the day's business. Master Tong's class had been going through their elegant motions for twenty minutes or so when the loud sound of screaming brakes was heard. A child had run in front of a delivery lorry. The lorry had turned sharply and fallen onto its side, trapping the driver, who had tried to jump clear. He was alive, but his legs were trapped under the lorry door. He was calling out for help and was obviously in great pain.

What happened next amazed Jamie. Master Tong ran to the lorry, took a deep breath and pushed up with both hands against the side of the lorry. What was the old man thinking of? What could he do? The lorry was not large but it was not something to be pushed away like an empty box.

But he lifted it up!

Master Tong held up the lorry while other willing hands pulled the driver away. Only after the driver was safe did he let go. The lorry sank down with a heavy sound of metal.

Master Tong sat down, a little red in the face but not hurt by his efforts. But Jamie had no time to talk to him as he was needed by the injured driver. He used his acupressure skills to reduce the poor man's pain until he could be taken to hospital. Jamie noticed a young woman by his side. It was the pretty woman from the *Tai Chi* class. She was busy talking to the injured man and helping him to relax. Their eyes met briefly and she smiled at him before she left to get more help.

When the ambulance arrived, Jamie saw that the *Tai Chi* class had begun again. People were gently moving in the new morning light, all following Master Tong.

*   *   *

The next day Jamie got to his *Tai Chi* class early. He wanted to speak to Master Tong before the class began.

Jamie saw him already doing his exercises next to a large banyan tree. Master Tong saw him and smiled.

'Always exercise next to a tree,' he said. 'Trees are good for the *chi*.'

Jamie looked at the slightly built man who was smiling at him. Could he really have moved that lorry by himself? Master Tong saw his face and answered for him.

'You need not be so surprised by what happened yesterday, my friend. You ought to know from your studies that the *chi* can be a practical tool, a way of finding outer as well as inner strength.'

'Yes, but I never thought . . . ' Jamie began.

Master Tong again seemed to read his mind. 'You never thought that a gentle form of exercise such as *Tai Chi* could produce such results, yes?'

'Well . . . er . . . yes,' answered Jamie.

'Observe,' said Master Tong.

Jamie saw him go through one of the more complicated exercises at the normal speed. The exercise involved movements that looked like elegant kicks and punches.

'Observe again,' Master Tong told him.

This time the exercise was performed much faster. Master Tong moved with a speed and power that took Jamie's breath away. There was nothing gentle about this!

'One side gentle, one side strong. Both are the same, both are part of the *chi*. You understand now?'

'I think so,' said Jamie.

'You used the gentle side of the *chi* yourself when you treated the injured man for his pain. That is good. We both use the *chi* when it is needed. That is balance. That is good. OK?'

Jamie nodded. He had seen something that would stay in his mind forever. He had seen strength as well as elegance.

He had also seen power and it was beautiful in his eyes.

* * *

It was a few months after Jamie's talk with Master Tong when Adrian approached Jamie. He and Jamie often talked together after work before they went home.

'My uncle tells me you are one of his best students,' Adrian told him.

'But I've only been with him for a few months!' said Jamie.

'Exactly! He says you've learned more in a few months than most do in a few years! How do you do it, Jamie?'

'Just lucky, I suppose,' said Jamie. They both laughed, but Jamie didn't add any more to explain his answer, though he wasn't sure why.

Adrian was too polite to ask again before he went home.

* * *

Jamie spent most of his time on studying and practising his skills. He would apply acupressure or sometimes needles to his skin in order to increase his *chi*. He needed more energy if he was to do all the things he wanted. And he wanted a lot.

Most of all he wanted power. He wanted the power of his *chi* to fill his being. He did not ask himself why he wanted it. He never questioned his desire for it, a desire that seemed to grow as naturally as his power grew.

But as his power grew his wisdom didn't.

Jamie was still doing well at the college. He was now head of the Business Studies department. The three other lecturers who were in the department liked Jamie, but he expected a lot from them. They wondered how he could work so hard. No matter how much they did, he always seemed to be doing more.

Jamie's department was becoming well-known for its excellent examination results. But his students, though they liked and respected Jamie, found that keeping up with all the work he wanted them to do was almost impossible. That is, if they expected to eat and sleep.

Jamie himself knew well enough that his expectations were beginning to be too much for his students and staff. He decided that something needed to be done about it. Of course! They could all join Master Tong's *Tai Chi* classes! Why not?

*   *   *

Jamie was feeling quite excited at the idea of his staff and students joining in the classes every morning. He never stopped to think that they might have other things to do with their lives; that they might have families to be with, or homes to look after or even other jobs to do.

He had not felt excited by anything in this way for some time. He was usually calm and in control of his feelings. He would speak to Master Tong about it tomorrow. But tonight he decided to walk home by way of the shopping centre, past all the bright shops and the colourful lights he had always found so cheerful. It was his way of celebrating.

But there were others who were also celebrating that night. And they were far from being calm. Five men were sitting at an outdoor table in a street café next to the pavement. They had been drinking too much beer. One of them saw Jamie walking past and called out to him.

'Hey, mate, do you speak English?'

Jamie looked at the man. He was big and was speaking too loudly.

'Yes,' said Jamie, politely. 'I *am* English. Can I help you?'

The men all shouted and laughed, repeating 'I *am* English' in a rude way that was meant to sound like him. Jamie ignored this.

'Yeah, mate, you can have a beer with us. It's my mate's birthday and I'm buying the drinks. You're my guest. You can drink to his health, too.'

'No thanks,' said Jamie. 'I don't drink beer, only water and tea.'

The other men all laughed loudly but the first man got angry.

'I'm not *asking* you, mate, I'm *telling* you. Now drink!'

The man pushed a beer can in front of Jamie's face. Jamie calmly turned away and began to walk off. He did not want to become involved with these men. The man reached out and roughly grabbed Jamie's shoulder.

Jamie did not even think about his next action. He turned quickly and pushed upwards with both hands against the man's chest. The man went up into the air and landed on another table, knocking over beer cans and breaking glasses. He did not get up.

Jamie could hardly believe what he had done. He had not meant to do anything violent. Now a man was hurt.

The four other men looked at the fallen man in horror. This quickly turned to anger as they got up and attacked

Jamie. They were all shouting angrily at him as they did so. Some had bottles in their hands and one had picked up a heavy wooden chair.

Jamie had not asked for this. He had not wanted to hurt anyone. Now four large drunken men were attacking him.

Something seemed to break inside Jamie's mind at that moment. It seemed to him as if the men were moving in slow motion. It was easy to avoid their punches, easy to hit them in places he knew would make them unconscious for a long time. It was just after the fourth man had gone down that he felt a sudden pain in his back. The floor rushed towards him. All the world went black and he knew no more.

*　　*　　*

Jamie's head hurt. He opened his eyes. The light hurt his eyes at first. He began to make out a face. It was the face of a woman. She was smiling at him. His eyes became more used to the light and he could see that the woman was a nurse. She had a nice face, a beautiful face. It seemed familiar.

'How are you feeling, Mr Russell?' the nurse asked.

'I feel awful,' said Jamie. 'My back hurts.'

'I'll get you something for the pain, Mr Russell. Just wait a moment.'

'No!' Jamie said with more force than he had intended. 'I don't need any drugs; just give me a minute.'

Only then did Jamie realise that he could not move his arms or legs. No matter how hard he tried to move, they remained still. He felt confused, sick and afraid.

'Please, Mr Russell, relax. I'll take care of things,' said

the nurse as she dried the sweat on his forehead. As she leaned over, Jamie saw from the badge she was wearing that her name was Angie Lee. Her hand was cool and her touch was light. She smiled at him. Then he remembered her – she was the pretty woman from the *Tai Chi* class who had helped the injured lorry driver! He managed to smile back.

'What happened, nurse? How did I get here?'

'Here is Doctor Sim. He'll tell you all you need to know, Mr Russell.'

Doctor Sim was a young man, younger than Jamie, but he spoke with the calm authority of a professional.

'A man hit a heavy chair against your backbone, Mr Russell. He injured your back and would have done more damage if the police hadn't arrived to stop him. It seems you got into a fight and put four of his friends into hospital before he did the same to you. Witnesses say the men started the trouble and you were trying to protect yourself. Rather well, too, until that chair hit you.'

'But I can't move my arms or legs!' cried Jamie.

'We don't want you to, Mr Russell; we have to keep your back still while it mends,' said Doctor Sim.

Jamie now realised that his whole body was being held still. Even his head was being held by something.

Doctor Sim continued: 'If you were to move now you could be damaged forever.'

'Forever!' Jamie heard the word but it did not seem real to him. Be calm, he told himself, be in control.

'Will I . . . will I get better?' he asked.

'Indeed you will,' said Doctor Sim. 'Providing you remain absolutely still for at least two months. We have to make sure your back mends fully before we can consider allowing you to move. But you should have made a full recovery by then, so don't worry. Enjoy the rest!'

Doctor Sim went on to his next patient.

Jamie felt that life had played a cruel trick on him. All that time spent on perfecting his body and his mind, and now he couldn't even get out of bed! He felt foolish and rather sorry for himself.

At that moment Nurse Angie Lee returned with some medicine for Jamie. He needed it.

*   *   *

After a few days he was allowed to see visitors. Adrian and Master Tong came to see him. Adrian talked about college and said how much Jamie was missed while Master Tong sat and said nothing. Adrian, after a nod from his uncle, then said goodbye and left.

Master Tong remained sitting by Jamie's bed, looking at him. Jamie wondered what he was thinking about but did not want to ask him. Finally, Master Tong spoke.

'I have been speaking to a friend of mine about you. He knows you well.'

'Yes? Who is that?'

'Mr Lo. He is concerned about you. You were his student once, I understand.'

'Why is he concerned?' asked Jamie. But he had a feeling he already knew.

'He could see something was happening to you. I could see it myself. I had hoped that the gentle side of your *chi* would correct the imbalance.'

'The imbalance?'

'Yes,' said Master Tong. 'The power of your *chi* was

rising up like a snake. You were losing control of it, upsetting the balance. Why else do you think you got into that ridiculous fight with those men? You have skill, but no wisdom. Why do you think it takes a lifetime to learn these things, eh? You want to know everything all at once! You think you can do everything by yourself! We could see that. But you are young. You can still learn. If you don't kill yourself first!'

And Master Tong laughed.

'I know you won't be able to move for a while, but they tell me you will make a good recovery. And if you use your *chi* you should recover even faster. Enjoy your rest. Now you have a chance to examine your mistakes, look at your life and consider how to balance your *chi* properly.'

Just then Nurse Angie Lee arrived and waited respectfully while Master Tong was speaking.

'And not all teachers are old men!' Master Tong continued. 'Your lessons begin now. I expect to see you back at my classes when you leave this place!'

Master Tong walked away. Jamie's eyes followed him as he walked through the door. Could Master Tong be right?

'Are you ready, Jamie?' said Nurse Angie. It was time for her to wash him. Jamie liked Nurse Angie's cheerful company. She seemed to like him. He knew he liked her. He liked her very much. She smiled at him and he smiled back.

Jamie closed his eyes and relaxed. Maybe Master Tong was right. Maybe his lessons were only just beginning.

He felt Angie's touch and it was cool and gentle.

Gentle as a feather.